D1241850

Published by Best Seller Publishing®, St. Augustine, FL
Best Seller Publishing® is a registered trademark.
Printed in the United States of America.

ISBN: 978-1-959840-75-6

Legal Notice

For more information, please write:
Best Seller Publishing®
53 Marine Street
St. Augustine, FL 32084
or call 1 (626) 765-9750
Visit us online at: www.BestSellerPublishing.org

CONTENTS

SECTION 3

DEDICATION

This book is dedicated to my amazing family—my wife, Tami, my daughter, Elexia, my son, Saxon, and my dog, Isla Joy.

A GIFT FOR YOU!

Download the free P.R.O.S.P.E.R. Formula spreadsheet at
http://prosperformula.com/resources

Take the free small business profit maximizer assessment
at http://prosperformula.com/assessment
Schedule your free strategy session with a P.R.O.S.P.E.R.
Formula Coach at https://prosperformula.com/strategy
Also get this FREE BONUS VIDEO TRAINING: ($297 Value)
P.R.O.S.P.E.R. Formula for Small Business
All yours FREE with this book.

DON'T WAIT!
Watch this FREE VIDEO TRAINING now, and
learn how to double your profit in 90 days.
http://prosperformula.com/resources

INTRODUCTION

STOP! I need you to do this first. Take your right hand, and reach high in the air. Now bend your arm at the elbow and pat the back part of your left shoulder. GREAT! That pat on the back was from me. You have taken an incredible first step by getting this book. The hardest part is over. You should be really excited about now. I'm getting goosebumps just thinking about it. Your business, your life, your world will not be the same in 120 days. I believe so much in the concepts and tactics of this book that I'll guarantee you will grow your business. All you must do is implement.

Though I strongly recommend that you read the entire book, I realize that we live in a microwave society with micro attention spans. So, for your convenience, I broke the book down into bite-sized sections where you can quickly find out how to solve the specific issues in your business. I fully expect you to highlight, underline, asterisk, dog-ear, and rip out the sections that apply to you. This is a workbook, with specific tactics and action steps.

If you were one of my consulting clients, the first thing I would do is audit your business and look for the weak points; every business has them. I would score you on the four circles of success, the customer journey, and on each ingredient in the P.R.O.S.P.E.R. Formula. Then we would get to work on making your weakness a strength.

In the first section of this book, I break down the four circles of success. This is a generalized overview of the four things every successful business must have. The second section of this book is the exact path you must take every customer along, on purpose. It's called the customer journey. When you do this, your business will grow dramatically. The third section in this book is the P.R.O.S.P.E.R. Formula; this is the specific steps you can take to double the profit of your business. If you implement any of the sections, your business will absolutely grow. The most successful businesses on earth are doing all of them.

In the past 30 years or so, as a student of marketing, I have interviewed more than 3,000 business owners from across the U.S. and Canada. I have sat knee to knee with most of them, but I have also been on the other end of the phone, or lately, the other side of Zoom. It truly fascinates me to hear the rags to riches stories of successful business owners.

When I was 20 years old, I was a DJ for a local radio station. The first success story I ever obtained was from the owner of a furniture store. He was a gangly man who could not read or write and probably had a big black spot on his liver from expensive single malt whiskey. This guy was incredibly resourceful. He bought an old abandoned elementary school because his old location did not have enough square footage for all his furniture. One summer Saturday, I was broadcasting live at his location, and because there is a lot of downtime in between breaks, I took up a conversation. I'm thankful my parents never taught me not to talk about money, because that's usually the first question out of my mouth. "This is quite the gig you have here; how much money do you make?" I asked. He smiled and said "millions," and it was easy to tell he wasn't lying. I asked him how he became successful with his "reading, writing" issues. He said that's exactly why he was successful. He couldn't get a regular job; no one would hire him. He started selling used stuff in the newspaper. He would dictate what to say in the ads to his sales rep. Slowly, over the years, he was able to open a storefront. Then, he got aggressive with his marketing. By the time I met him, he had three locations. He dominated the local newspapers, radio stations, TV, and billboards. Also, he dabbled in direct mail, Yellow Pages, and even urinal signs. People would come from over 100 miles away to shop at his stores. My next question to him was, *Why?*

Why come here over the other ten furniture stores in the area? He called it *train wreck marketing*. "They hear or see my crazy marketing ads, and they always think 'It's too good to be true.' People must come just to see what it is all about, and then when they get here, I actually over-deliver on my promises," he proclaimed. "Integrity is everything, especially for someone with no pedigree. People do business with people they know, like, and trust. All I had to do was get more people to know me, get them to like me, and prove I'm trustworthy." That was the first time I had ever heard this simple but effective formula for business success.

From that moment on, this has been the litmus test for every business I interview. I always ask, "How do you get more people to know you, how do you get them to like and trust you?" Every single successful business owner I've asked this question has had a specific answer. None of them were "winging" it. They all have a plan on how to get more people to know them, then get them to like and trust them. On the contrary, the non-successful businesses I interviewed didn't have a plan. They would usually answer, "Word of mouth is our best form of advertising," and I knew it was a matter of time before their doors would close.

Eventually, I discovered the rest of the formula to success that all successful businesses follow, knowingly or unknowingly.

Here is the exact path to success in business. This is the journey you must take with each customer: Know, Like, Trust, Try, Buy, Evangelize. We will go over all of these in extensive detail.

P.R.O.S.P.E.R. Formula

I love the words *prosper* and *prosperous*. I use those words in three of my businesses because I want all our clients to have a prosperous journey.

Prosper biblically comes from the Greek word *euodoō*, which means to grant a successful issue, to succeed in an enterprise or activity, to succeed in business affairs, be successful, thrive, advance in any good thing, render happy, favorable, fortunate, succeed in reaching; figuratively, a prosperous journey.

Beloved, I wish above all things that thou mayest prosper and be in health, even as thy soul prospereth. —*III John 1:2*

Formula–recipe, prescription, blueprint, pattern, conventional method for doing something: procedure to be followed to get a predictable result.

I consider myself a curator of business success tactics. Each year, I read or listen to at least thirty non-fiction books about business, success, mindset, leadership, and so on, and I file the best tactics from each book. I also attend three to five business conferences per year, in which I take notes from spectacular speakers and monumentally successful business owners. This book you are about to read is a culmination of everything I have learned over the past three decades in working with highly successful businesses, reading the books, and taking the training. There is nothing new under the sun, but I think you will see the way I package the content is quite unique and easily implementable. That's my entire goal of this book. I want you to implement.

I have worked arduously to make the tactics as concise as possible, and I put them into an easily entreated formula.

By the end of this book, you will be able to employ this formula and shortcut success. There may be other paths, but none as succinct and predictable as this one. It's a formula, a recipe if you will, that has some room for creative autonomy but ultimately, if followed, will deliver a decadent meal every single time. This is the only book you will need to catapult you and your business to prosperity.

SECTION 1

CHAPTER 1

FOUR CIRCLES OF SUCCESS
(Mindset-Skill Set-Toolset-
Get Off Your Asset)

Success Leaves Clues.

—Jim Rohn

S uccess absolutely, positively, leaves clues. As a matter of fact, in every industry, in every niche, there are probably dozens or hundreds of successful companies you can specifically, strategically, learn from. There are also hundreds of average or failing businesses where you can learn what NOT to do. In today's world, with all our technological advances, it's almost effortless to reverse engineer a competitor. Throughout this book, I'm going to give you the tactical action steps that you can take to see exactly how your competition became successful and why they continue to be successful. All you need to do is swipe, make it your own, and deploy.

I'll tell you right now that there are really only four things any successful person or successful company does to be successful. When you break each of these four circles down—and truly buy into the philosophy and the psychology, systemize the processes, implement the standard operating procedures, get the right tools that you need, and take massive action—you will have no choice but to be successful.

In the past couple of decades, there have been massive advancements in psychotherapy, specifically, cognitive behavior therapy (CBT). We can definitely see powerful transformation when doctors help individuals with their cognitions (mental activities like thoughts, beliefs, values, memories, and the like) and behaviors (things you do). The CBT triangle is thoughts, feelings, and behaviors. All three are powerfully intertwined and create either an upward spiral or a downward spiral. Your thoughts create feelings, your feelings create behavior, behavior reinforces thoughts. Astonishingly, it works backward as well. By changing your behaviors, you can change your feelings, which change your thoughts. Psychologists learned long ago that lasting change must come from changing all three: thoughts, feelings, and behaviors. My entire objective and mission of this book is to do exactly that—change your thoughts, feelings, and behaviors.

Just like the CBT triangle, the four circles of success are intertwined and each one builds upon the others. Interestingly we find it similar that once you move forward in one area, the other three areas will come along. The shortcut to success is to start with one of them, just one. We need to intervene and disrupt the status quo of just one of these circles, which in turn will trigger the others. I call it the upward spiral (keeping with the circle theme).

For instance, let's say you see an ad for new software for your business. It looks powerful and like everything you need. It can help systematize your processes, organize your database, and even bring in new inbound leads. The software has a hefty price, but you decide to take the risk and buy it anyway. Now you have skin in the game, and your thought patterns have immediately changed from being stuck in a rut to new beliefs and a new motive to take action to learn and implement the software.

As you take action and you are learning how to implement and optimize the software, you gain new skills. Then, your beliefs continue to change because you can visualize how this software will help your business, which in turn inspires you to take more action. The success pattern is now in motion, and it will continue to build until something with equal or greater force stops it. It is like Newton's first law of motion: "An object in motion stays in motion with the same speed and in the same direction unless acted upon by an unbalanced force."

This is relevant to our circles of success. Once we are in motion, we can be defined by our velocity, which is speed with a direction. Then inertia takes over, which is the tendency of an object to resist changes in its velocity.

Unfortunately, there can also be other scenarios with much different outcomes. Let us say you buy that new software, and you investigate implementing it, but it's cumbersome and complex. You get stuck in the setup, which is disheartening and frustrating (feelings). You send in a support ticket to the help desk with no response, and you are stuck (thoughts). You give up, and it sits there for a month until you get your second billing. This really stings because you are nowhere even close to implementing the software, so you cancel your subscription (behavior). Newton's first law also says: "An object at rest stays at rest." An object at rest has zero velocity and will remain at zero velocity unless we take action.

If I'm being honest, I have definitely had both of the scenarios in my business, even recently. Maybe you have too.

Over the next four chapters, we will dissect each of the circles to success so we can better understand the power of each of them individually and the synergy within all of them. We will begin each chapter in the rest of this book with a 30,000-foot, high-level vantage to compile insight and get a foundational grasp on the concepts. Then, we will go in the trenches and discuss specific strategies, tactics, and action steps and exactly how to implement them. The four circles to success are Mindset, Skill Set, Toolset, and Get Off Your Asset. Let's start with Mindset.

CHAPTER 2

MINDSET
(Beliefs, Attitudes, Thoughts, Your Paradigm)

Eighty percent of success is due to psychology—mindset, beliefs, and emotions—and only twenty percent is due to strategy—the specific steps needed to accomplish a result.
—Anthony Robbins

30K FOOT VIEW

Undoubtedly, mindset is critical to any success. In fact, successful entrepreneurs must believe in themselves, in their businesses, and in their products or services. They must also believe in their ability to succeed. And most of all, they understand the power of beliefs to determine what they will or will not do, what they will or will not tolerate, and the actions they will or will not take. It's a choice; sometimes you just have to change your mind. Henry Ford once said, "If you think you can do a thing or think you can't do a thing … you're right."

I get it, trust me. I know that it's much easier said than done. Sometimes when the *fit hits the shan*, it's much easier to throw your hands up and say "See, I knew it!" than it is to push through and find a way. Successful people have some head trash from time to time, just like all of us do, but they get control of their thinking and focus on solving the problems at hand. That's how they move ahead.

A wise man from Philly once said, "Let me tell you something you already know. The world ain't all sunshine and rainbows. It's a very mean and nasty place, and I don't care how tough you are, it will beat you to your knees and keep you there permanently if you let it. You, me, or nobody is gonna hit as hard as life. But it ain't about how hard you hit, it's about how hard you can get hit and keep moving forward. How much you can take and keep moving forward. That's how winning is done!"

Your mindset is a collection of habitual thoughts and attitudes that shape your innermost beliefs. Your innermost beliefs are called your personal paradigm or your identity. Your personal paradigm is your way of looking at a situation—how you perceive it and understand it from your perspective. Your paradigm completely directs how you see yourself and the lens through which you see the world around you. It's your frame of reference that contains your basic assumptions, your innermost beliefs, your ways of thinking, and your methodology of reasoning.

> *Your mind is a garden. Thoughts are the seeds of your words*
> *and deeds. You can grow fruit, or you can grow weeds.*
> *—William Wordsworth*

It's like the tale of the two shoe salespeople who were sent to a third-world country to sell shoes. When the first one got there, he called back to the office and said, "Get me a plane ticket home. This is useless. No one wears shoes around here." The second salesperson looked around and called and said, "Send me all the shoes you have. No one has shoes around here!"

Your mindset is a psychological outlook that predetermines your interpretation and your responses to every situation. Your identity is your beliefs, your mindset in which you hold, which drives your actions that you take and the results you get. Your mindset absolutely skews reality, either positive or negative. Rarely do we have thoughts or make decisions that come from a neutral mindset. Our pre-programmed mindset will set the tone for every situation.

> *For as he thinketh in his heart, so is he.*
> *—Proverbs 23:7a*

To profoundly change your mindset, you must change your heart, your innermost beliefs, your paradigm.

Unfortunately, mindsets are deeply ingrained into our neural pathways, and it requires a diligent effort to change them. Donald Hebb's discovery in 1949 tells us that "Neurons that fire together wire together." This is a process of forming, strengthening, and solidifying neural pathways. Science tells us that neural plasticity is a physical change to the pathways in your brain. These pathways are molded and shaped every day by our experiences and thought patterns. To create new pathways in our brain, we must upset the status quo by changing our thoughts, feelings, and behaviors to specific stimuli. In short, we must change our personal paradigm. We can change these automatic reactions, thoughts, and behaviors by consciously and repeatedly adjusting the way we view that stimuli and ultimately by changing our response to those stimuli.

It's sort of like a biking trail. Just as the path gets worn down by all the tires trekking the same area over and over, the grass gets flattened and worn away. Over the days, months, and years, that pathway is well solidified and easily journeyed. It becomes the easy route, the path of least resistance. Fortunately, or unfortunately as the case may be, as you practice traveling down new pathways and neglect your old pathways, those old pathways naturally weaken. The new pathway becomes the easy route.

IN THE TRENCHES
Four Steps to Changing Your Mindset

People are just as happy as they make up their minds to be.
—Usually attributed to Abraham Lincoln

Dr. Stephen R. Covey, author of one of the most prolific and influential business books of the twentieth century, titled *The 7 Habits of Highly Effective People*, tells us that "Every human has four unique endowments. 1.) Self-awareness 2.) Conscience 3.) Creative Imagination and 4.) Independent will or volition. These four endowments give us the ultimate human freedom, the power to choose, to respond, to change." Dr. Covey is telling us that, because of these four unique human endowments, we have the power within us to change our minds.

The first step in changing our mindset is self-awareness. Self-awareness is a huge, vital step in changing our mindset. It is the conscious knowledge of our character, our thoughts, our feelings, motives, and beliefs. To actually change our mindset, we must deliberately focus on the inner conversations we have with ourselves. We must purposefully and consistently be aware of our thoughts and take control of them. In 2005, the National Science Foundation published an article summarizing research on human thoughts per day. It was found that the average person has about 12,000 thoughts per day, and intellectuals have up to 60,000 thoughts per day. Most business owners fall somewhere in the middle. (A related side study showed that politicians had up to 17 thoughts a day, all related to spending more taxpayers' money, but I digress.) Of the thousands of thoughts we have per day, scientists say up to a staggering 80 percent of them are negative. That could seem almost incomprehensible to me until I take inventory of my own thoughts for a day.

The same scientists also report that 95 percent of our thoughts were basically the same repetitive thoughts as the day before. Unfortunately, if gone unchecked, our mind tends to dwell on the negatives, repeatedly.

The severe form of this is called perseveration, which is the uncontrolled repetition or continuation of a response (motor act, word, thought, activity, strategy, or emotion) that has persisted beyond the psychological context or rationale in which it arose.

Unlike animals, all humans have the aptitude for cognitive time travel. Sometimes we dwell on negative experiences from the past, but mostly we have predictive negative thoughts of the future like doubt, worry, and fear. As the adage goes, "If doubt, worry, and fear were liquor, wine, and beer, some people would be drunk every day of their lives."

To overcome all this negative talk, we need to be cognizant of our thoughts in every pertinent situation. We need to be "self-aware." Knowledge is power, and consequently self-knowledge is self-empowerment. This statement is so profound that I think you need to read it again. Knowledge is power, and consequently self-knowledge is self-empowerment!

After we are aware of our thoughts, the second step in changing our mindset is to objectively evaluate these thoughts, feelings, beliefs, and actions as to whether or not they serve us. This is called "conscious evaluation." We get to decide if these thoughts are right or wrong according to our goals, morals, values, and principles. Our conscience is more than just gut instinct; our conscience is a moral muscle. This is easier said than done because we are uniquely biased and subjective to our experiences. Dr. Covey further explains our conscious evaluation like this: "In the space between stimulus (what happens) and how we respond, lies our freedom to choose. Ultimately, this power to choose is what defines us as human beings. We may have limited choices, but we can always choose. We can choose our thoughts, emotions, moods, our words, our actions; we can choose our values and live by principles. It is the choice of acting or being acted upon."

That space between stimulus and response is unique to humans. I have a beautiful, all-black German shepherd. If I smacked her upside the head, her only response could be fight, flight, or freeze. (Don't worry, I've never tried it, so I don't know what her response would be, but it would be one of those.) The sympathetic nervous system drives the fight, flight, freeze response. But if I smacked you upside the head, you would have the same three options and dozens more. You could choose to laugh; you could turn the other cheek. You could whistle the theme song to *The Andy Griffith Show*.

Unfortunately, if gone unchecked, humans can turn on the fight, flight, or freeze response just by thought alone. That thought doesn't have to be about anything happening presently. We can turn on that response by anticipation or revisiting an unhappy memory.

To be consciously aware is simply to be self-aware with the added action of choosing the best thoughts and actions in any given situation.

The third step in changing our mindset is using our creative imagination to create a new path in our mind before we can do it in reality. This is where we consciously override our entrenched predictive negative thoughts with new ones that better serve us. We visualize the future, can see it in detail, and can imagine what it will be like. My dog can't do that either.

On a side note, those who attempt to exercise creative imagination without conscience, inevitably create the unconscionable.

As we learned earlier, by default, our imagination tends to lean toward negative thoughts of the future like doubt, worry, and fear. We must consciously control our vision of the future to line up with the positive results we want. We must visualize success and the specific action steps it will take to get us there. If visualized enough, it will eventually get easier and easier, until it's the path of least resistance.

Lastly, the fourth step in changing our mindset is exercising our independent free will. Free will or volition is our God-given freedom to make a decision or choice after deliberation and act upon it in the manner in which we choose, that which is most appropriate.

We must choose to be self-aware and consciously evaluate, and then we must visualize a successful future and finally take specific deliberate actions on our new beliefs. And that's exactly how we change our mindset! This is akin to riding our bike off the beaten path and making a new route. At first, this will undoubtedly be much harder. But it will make for a much more enjoyable ride and certainly a better destination.

One of the most paramount things I get to do each year is help lead a youth leadership camp. It's four days in the woods with 75+ tenth graders. We immerse them in over a hundred initiatives (games with a purpose) that intentionally teach leadership skills. One of the most humbling initiatives is affectionately called the "Pamper Pole." It's a 30 foot telephone pole that the students climb, then jump off. Of course, they wear a safety harness, and they are safely caught by a tethered rope before they peril to the ground. It got its name because there is an unusual substantial percentage of the students, boys and girls alike, that cry like a baby climbing up the pole.

A few years ago, when my daughter was in the tenth grade, she was invited to the camp and found herself at the base of the pole. She had heard rumors of course, and in years prior, she heard me talk about some of the big tough football players who were quickly humbled by the pole and had to climb back down, failing to complete the initiative. My slightly stubborn and persistent daughter put on her big-girl smile and started to climb. Her team was cheering her on, and she was doing great until that last step up to stand with both feet on top of the swaying pole. It was that last step where she froze, and tears started rolling like Niagara Falls. You see, my daughter had it in her mind that she was going to make me proud; that she was going to jump off that pole. However, reality slapped her hard, and sheer panic and fear stopped her in her place. My absolute favorite quote from Mike Tyson is relevant here. He said, "Everyone has a plan until they get punched in the mouth."

What seemed like eternity to her encouraging teammates must have felt even longer to my daughter. She wrestled with her mind and fought with her fears as she stood there, shaking, with one foot atop the pole. Finally, unexpectedly, after three minutes and twenty-one seconds of her being frozen in that position, she stepped up. I know this because it's on video. You can see her demeanor completely change. Her tenacity kicked in, and she fought back the tears and bravely stepped up with both feet on top of that pole. She raised her arms in victory and after regaining her composure, she jumped and hit the ball ten feet out, effectively signifying her completion of the initiative. She was safely hoisted to the ground where her teammates and camp leaders all joyously congratulated her.

I asked her over and over what was going through her mind. She said, "I wanted to step up, but I couldn't; the pole was shaking too much." I said, "What changed when you finally did step up?" She said, "The pole stopped shaking."

What I think happened was she got control of her fears, became self-aware, and changed her thinking from "I can't do this" to "I can do this." She became consciously aware of her situation. She changed her mind from fear and reasoned that since she was in a safety harness, if she fell, she wouldn't get hurt. Then, through creative imagination, she visualized each move that would get her victory. She imagined herself on top of that pole and ultimately victorious. Once she had control of her mindset, her body once again was subject to her mind. She was now in control of her independent free will, and she decided to move her foot up to the top of the pole. She successfully and purposefully changed her mind. As her father, I could not have been prouder.

This is exactly what we can do to change our mindset. We can deliberately, intentionally, and purposefully go through these four steps to changing our mindset, and we too can have that victory. Fortunately for us, we are probably not 30 feet off the ground when we must make these life-altering decisions.

CHAPTER 3

SKILL SET
(Abilities, Aptitude, Competency, Techniques, Proficiency, Training)

30K FOOT VIEW

A skill is the ability to perform an activity in a competent manner. Over the years, many gurus and experts have separated out different skills into easy-to-swallow categories, like soft skills and hard skills. Soft skills are things like communication and interpersonal skills, leadership skills, problem-solving skills; even emotional intelligence is a soft skill. Hard skills are more specific physical skills like welding, design, juggling, bookkeeping, foreign languages, playing the guitar, and computer programming. Throughout our life, we all have mastered hundreds of skills, everything from driving to tying our shoes to making coffee to golfing (well, no one has truly mastered golfing). In the book *Outliers*, Malcolm Gladwell contends that a person could become world class if they put in over ten thousand hours of deliberate practice. Deliberate is defined as purposeful and systematic practicing in such a way that it pushes your skill set, with the specific goal of improvement. Though most psychologists say this theory is way oversimplified, they all agree that hard and soft skills are a "learned" trait. No one is born with the amazing ability to hit a five iron or program an app or pick a banjo. Those skills must be learned through hundreds, maybe thousands of hours of deliberate practice. The good news for you and me is we have the ability to learn almost whatever skill we put our minds to. Even better news is that to be great at most of our professions takes way less than 10,000 hours (most small business owners don't need to be world class, just great). And the best news of all is you are probably already 90 percent of the way there. All you really need to do is solidify your direction and make some minor tweaking by adjusting your execution over and over and putting in the work.

The fastest and most sure way to better your skills is by having an accountability partner or coach. You need someone who will show you the path, establish your goals with you, and hold you accountable.

My son has played baseball for over a dozen years since he was five. He has played on numerous travel ball teams and placed very well in national showcases. I've had countless coaches and parents compliment him on his "natural talents." I think they mean well, but it's almost an insult to how hard he has worked to get those "natural talents." I used to hit tennis balls to him as hard as I possibly could hundreds of times every day. At first, the ball would pop out all the time (tennis balls are much harder to squeeze in the glove because they are so bouncy). I could spin it and trick him. He'd miss the short hop or the backhand, or it would bounce up and hit him in the chest. It wasn't long before he would make those amazing catches, pick the short hop, spin, and throw it back at me. Now in a game, it's second nature. He is a vacuum. He makes it look easy and natural. Behind the scenes, I saw firsthand what it took to be great. It took thousands of hours of practice before he could do this consistently at an elite level. Yes, my son has some natural talents, but he's amazing on defense and offense because he has thrown, caught, and hit the ball tens of thousands of times. He had deliberate practice with the intent on getting better. It's a skill he developed, strategically and on purpose. You could do the exact same in your field of play.

Odds are, if you are reading this book, you are physically and mentally capable of being world class in your profession.

Nowadays, there really is no excuse for not excelling at your trade. Everything is available at our fingertips or thumb tips. I'm willing to bet that no matter what your profession or business, you have no less than fifty books or as many training courses, videos, articles, white papers, and associations you could join, dozens of apps, dozens of personal trainers or coaches, and at least a half dozen live events you could attend to deliberately help yourself grow and get better. If not, you certainly need to write a book and become a coach because it's needed in every industry. The only thing holding you back from being world class (or at least state class or top of your town class) is you and the extent of your tenacity in honing your skills.

IN THE TRENCHES

If you are thinking, "What skill(s) should I develop?" Let me give you some ideas. In general, soft skills will serve you the rest of your life no matter what profession or business you choose to be in. I strongly recommend deliberate practice in honing your communication skills. One hundred percent of all successful people are excellent at communicating either in writing or orally, or both. I remember when I was trying to choose a major in college, my advisor said *go for communications; it's used in every business*. I'm so thankful I did. My communications degree has served me very well in over ten different professions and businesses I have owned.

Steve Jobs understood that spoken communication was the key to Apple's success. Unfortunately, he was horrible at speaking on stage. He practiced deliberately for dozens of hours offstage, and dozens more hours onstage, in an empty auditorium to get his speeches down. Those closest to him knew he believed there was nothing more important than his MacWorld keynotes. Those speeches set the entire tone for the brand and sold billions of dollars in merchandise for the company.

Oral and written communication can catapult you to success as well. I recommend you join a local Toastmasters group or local networking clubs so that you can practice speaking in front of an audience. The value you'll get will be worth a hundred times the time and money you put in. If you are already a good speaker, volunteer to speak at the local chamber or Rotary clubs. This will help you practice speaking and get you in front of your peers.

Other soft skills I recommend you learn are leadership skills and emotional intelligence skills. You should be quite proficient in motivating, encouraging, persuading, and inspiring others. You should also learn humility, learn to be creative, and to think analytically, and you should be able to empathize with others. Yes, just like communicating, all these skills can be deliberately learned and greatly improved.

One hard skill that I think is mandatory to excel at if you are a business owner or entrepreneur is marketing. I believe it's absolutely vital to your success, especially in today's business environment. We will dig deep into the hard skill of marketing later in this book. You will learn powerful things that you can implement right away and see verifiable results.

Other obvious hard skills you should master are things to make your life more efficient and effective. Things like typing (not three-finger poking), time-blocking, scheduling, interviewing, hiring, onboarding, training, troubleshooting, managing, writing standard operating procedures, bookkeeping, and so on. All these traits are mandatory in scaling any successful business. A quick Google search will render dozens of classes, books, and videos on how to master each of these hard and soft skills. My advice is to cancel your Netflix and Hulu accounts and buy Audible and Udemy subscriptions.

CHAPTER 4

TOOLSET
(Hardware-Software)

30K FOOT VIEW

If skill set is simply a map showing you where to find the gold, then the toolset is the shovel, pickaxe, backhoe, bulldozer, and metal detector that will help make it easier and more efficient for you to dig for the gold.

Software and hardware are the cheat codes to the game of success. They allow you to skip over pitfalls, defeat your foes, speed up production, leapfrog your competition, minimize waste, and maximize your most valuable asset: your time.

If we go back in history, it is easy to see how tools accelerated success. The Industrial Revolution (mid-1800s–1830) dramatically increased the wealth of the individual, the wealth of businesses, and the wealth of the nation. It mechanized and systematized manufacturing, and radically increased production. Every single aspect of life was improved. People had access to better healthcare and healthier diets, better housing, better transportation, and cheaper goods all around.

The Second Industrial Revolution (1870–1914), also known as the Technological Revolution, was the phase of rapid standardization. Technology was standardized so as to make it much easier to mass produce and systematize. This allowed things like the railroad, telegraph, electric, water, sewage, gas, and many other technological systems to have enormous advancement and expansion throughout the United States and the world. These tools massively sped up production, increased the rate of growth and change, vastly decreased costs, and catapulted our nation into unprecedented economic growth.

We saw the same thing happen in the Digital Revolution, also known as the Third Industrial Revolution (late 1940s–2016). The Digital Revolution converted technology that had been analog into a digital format. By doing this, it became possible to make copies that were identical to the original with zero loss of integrity. Of equal importance, the new digital formats gave the ability to easily move digital information between media and allowed remote access to it.

The Digital Revolution brought along with it personal computers and ultimately the World Wide Web, which is the beginning of the Information Age.

Contrary to the ridiculous inferred notion that Al Gore invented the internet, it was actually a British scientist named Tim Berners-Lee who invented the World Wide Web (WWW) in 1989. This made it quick and easy to access modernized information and become the driving force of social evolution. The world quickly became a global village.

By 2010, cell phones with access to the internet (smartphones), became as ubiquitous as personal computers, and therefore almost ALL known information is now literally thumb tips away.

In 2016, we crossed into the Fourth Industrial Revolution, with the blurring of boundaries between the physical, digital, and biological worlds. It's a combination of advances in artificial intelligence (AI), robotics, the Internet of Things (IoT), 3D printing, genetic engineering, quantum computing, and other technologies. The tools we have available today are magnificent.

Let's bring this back to how this specifically helps you and your business to become successful. Make no mistake about it, you absolutely need tools to be successful; that's why it's one of the four circles to success. But which tools? You have an exorbitant number of choices of available tools at your fingertips that could potentially catapult your business.

The conundrum is the high possibility that we get caught up yearning after the new, improved, lustrous, glitzy, exceedingly polished, metallic doodad. This is known as magpie syndrome or SOS (shiny object syndrome). We can also fall prey to FOMO (fear of missing out), which is another strong motivator for purchasing new tools. "Everyone else is doing it! I should too!" The dilemma is deciding which tools to hitch our wagon to, and even more troubling, which ones we shouldn't. My advice is, once again, success leaves clues. In your industry, there are dozens of phenomenally successful businesses that you should learn from. Subtract the outliers, those who threw a "Hail Mary" and luckily become successful. You want to emulate the staples, the blue chips. What software do they use? What are their standard operating procedures? What exactly do they sell, and at what cost? What systems are they using? How are they marketing their business?

Amazingly, most successful businesses will happily divulge these things if you just ask.

As far as marketing goes, within minutes you can reverse engineer someone in your niche who is extraordinarily successful. If you are a plumbing/HVAC contractor in Baltimore, you could easily find the most successful contractor in Denver and literally swipe and deploy the same business plan and same marketing in your market. You could design your website similar to theirs, have the same slogan, same standard operating procedures. You wouldn't need to reinvent or trial by error anything because the path to success has already been formed and proven. This is the exact same reason franchises have an 85 percent success rate after five years. They share valuable inside information on what works and what doesn't. All you have to do is follow the formula. In most sectors, franchises have almost 20 percentage points higher success rate than individual operators. I'm not necessarily advocating for you to buy a franchise. I am, however, strongly suggesting that you don't need to reinvent the wheel. The internet is a powerful tool for you to search and research how to make your specific business successful.

Tim Ferris, the author of *The 4-Hour Workweek*, also wrote a mammoth of a book called *Tools of Titans*. This explicitly lays out amazing insight into the tools, tactics, routines, and habits of billionaires, icons, and world-class performers. There is a definite pattern to success, and I recommend you learn from the greats.

IN THE TRENCHES

Almost every day, certainly a couple of times every week, I will reverse engineer what a prospective client is doing online; then I compare that with their local competitors. I simply call this a marketing strategy session.

Let me walk you through some of the tools I use to do this. It will undoubtably help you and your business.

Let's start with Google. For obvious reasons, Google is the 800-pound gorilla. There is a reason Google became the fourth company to reach a market capitalization of a trillion dollars (behind Apple, Amazon, and Microsoft). As of mid-2022, Google is responsible for 92 percent of all searches worldwide. That's 3.5 billion searches a day, or 40,000 searches a second. Almost all information flows through Google (sort of scary when you think about it, isn't it?) Until October 2015, Google's motto was "Don't be evil." Following Google's corporate restructuring to Alphabet, Inc., they took "Do the right thing" as their motto. How much evil they do and whose opinion of what is right is up for debate. But I digress—here's where Google is excellent at helping your business.

To understand Google, you must understand the basis of their operating system. Google uses an extremely complicated algorithm to serve up search results. In fact, Google uses a highly advanced machine-learning artificial intelligence system called RankBrain to help sort through its search results. Google has confirmed there are over 300 major ranking signals which are evaluated that, in turn, might have up to 10,000 variations or sub-signals. Suffice it to say, it's complicated, but at its core it is just math. My advice is to win the math. In general more is better.

Here are some Google Apps your business should absolutely be using. Don't just skip over these. Remember, the right tools will undoubtably catapult your business.

1. **Google Analytics:** an essential tool for any small business. Knowledge is power, especially with online marketing. Google Analytics makes it extremely easy to see granular information about your website, your traffic, customer locations, their behaviors, keywords, conversions, and more. Sadly, almost 50 percent of local businesses don't have this free measurement tool installed on their website. This tells me they are not looking at vital metrics to win online. In fact, I have yet to find a dominant player in any market that isn't measuring their online activity. https://analytics. google.com

2. **Google My Business:** I read an article from Google a few years back that says over 30 percent of local business listings are not claimed. I sure hope it's not that high anymore, but just in case, make sure your business is claimed. https://www.google.com/ business/. I think the confusion comes in because Google will automatically make you a free listing and most of the info is usually correct. Many business owners see their listing and think they are good to go. But if you have not received an automated phone call from Google with a five-digit pin or a postcard in the mail with a pin, you are not verified. Once you are verified, fill out everything, I mean everything. It will ask you what category of business you are in. Make sure it's the closest category you can find. For instance, if you are a lawyer, don't just select "attorney" as your category; that's too broad. Pick "personal injury attorney." Then your secondary category could be "attorney" or "law firm." Make sure you fill out your hours of operations, your services, your products, and your

service area. Upload photos of the outside, inside, and employees and customers, and upload video walkthroughs and customer testimonials. Add types of payments, the date you opened, and so on. Make sure you fill out everything. Remember, this is a free service from Google. They often reward businesses who fill out more of their profile by ranking them higher in the maps, which is exactly what you want.

3. **Google Search Console:** helps you monitor, maintain, and troubleshoot your site's presence in Google search results. You can also confirm that Google can find and crawl your site, see how many pages are indexed, fix indexing problems, and request re-indexing of new or updated content. https://search.google.com/search-console/about.

4. **Google Tag Manager:** Manage tags without editing your site code. This is a critical tool that makes it extremely easy to install tracking conversions as well as analytics and other measurements tools and JavaScript tags on your website.

5. **Google PageSpeed Insights:** This will show you the speed of your website for desktop and mobile. It also shows you how to speed it up. Speed matters to Google, especially on mobile. According to Google, 53 percent of people will abandon a mobile website if it takes longer than three seconds to load. That's why they make it an important ranking factor on mobile. https://developers.google.com/speed/pagespeed/insights/

    Here's a non-Google website speed test.

    (https://gtmetrix.com is another great website speed tester.)

6. **"Google" this: "Site:yourcompetitorswebsite.com":** This will give you a snapshot of every page that Google has put into its main index. Sometimes it's eye-opening how many pages your competitors have, even ones hidden from the main menu.

7. **Google your phone number**: You will be amazed at what you will find, especially if you have been around for many years. I routinely find a ton of misinformation like wrong addresses, wrong hours, wrong websites, and so on. You should clean all of this up.

8. **Google your business name:** Go through every page looking for citations. Citations are simply other websites citing your name, address, phone number, website, and so on. Often, they are directories, but citations could come from dozens of diverse types of websites. This is extremely helpful in getting a baseline of your backlinks. All top ranked websites have dozens, maybe even hundreds or thousands of citations. You could easily sign up for twenty a day, and it would be worth the effort. While you are there, make sure all the information is correct on each one and fill it out completely. For a quick list of some of the top citations, go to https://prosperousim.com/citations.

9. **Google your business name (again):** Look for all the reviews you can find. Of course, you will see your Google My Business reviews, but all the other reviews will show up in the search as well, and some are deeply buried. Many business owners don't realize they have rogue bad reviews online. This is something you should continually monitor. I would argue that your online reputation is even more important than your offline reputation. Behind Google, the top secondary review sites are as follows:

> Facebook
> Yelp.com
> Yellowpages.com
> Better Business Bureau
> TripAdvisor.com
> CitySearch.com
> Angieslist.com
> Manta.com

Foursquare.com

Superpages.com

Glassdoor.com

Trustpilot.com

Avvo.com (legal)

10. **Google your top competitors' names and phone number:** You should look at their reviews and citations. Also look for anomalies: listings where you could be listed as well.

Other online marketing tools you should be using:

1. **Website audits:** These are essential to see what Google sees when they look at your site. They also help you compare your site to competitors'. My favorite website audit tools are https://Semrush.com and https://ahrefs.com, https://cognitiveseo.com/site-audit/. They all give you a nice recap of all your pages and any issues. It will quickly show you dead links, missing tags, (like header, description, alt tag) misspellings, and a few dozen other useful insights. I also use these audits on competitors' websites to see what they have going on behind the scenes.

2. **Other search engine optimization (SEO) tools:**
   https://moz.com/free-seo-tools has some great free measurement tools.
   https://semrush.com/
   https://majestic.com/
   https://cognitiveseo.com/
   https://www.screamingfrog.co.uk/
   https://semalt.com/

3. **Pay-per-click analysis:**

https://spyfu.com spy on your competitors and see how much they are spending on PPC (pay-per-click). This tool is rarely accurate but usually close enough. It will highlight who the players are and what their ads say.

4. **Technology lookup:** See what apps, software, and hosting your competitors are using.

https://builtwith.com/

https://www.nerdydata.com/

https//whois.domaintools.com/

5. **Dynamic call tracking:** Alternate phone numbers are used for tracking individual marketing. You can now definitively see where your leads are coming from online. I say, in God we trust, in all others we must see the hard data. You absolutely need to be tracking the results of your marketing.

https://VocalCola.com This one is by far the best and cheapest. Yes, I am biased because I am a co-owner. But the reason we developed it was because we were spending a fortune using other call tracking software without getting nearly the same amount of data.

Dynamic call tracking numbers should be used for all online marketing efforts. This is where the phone number is dynamically inserted into your website depending on where the lead originates from. This allows you to measure your return on ad spend (ROAS). This is a mission critical metric or KPI (key performance indicator). Reason being, once you realize how much it costs to get a lead, you can ultimately find out how much it costs to make a sale. You can, with confidence, scale your business. As one of the godfathers of marketing, Dan Kennedy, says, "The company that can spend the most to acquire a customer wins."

6. **Customer relationship management (CRM) tools:** CRM tools are necessary for all small businesses. Customer relationship management is the process of managing interactions with existing as well as past and potential customers.

   https://www.salesforce.com/
   https://monday.com/
   https://www.hubspot.com/
   https://www.freshworks.com/
   https://www.zoho.com/
   https://www.pipedrive.com/
   https://www.vcita.com/

   Niche-Specific CRM:
   https://gohighlevel.com/ Marketing Agencies
   https://www.servicetitan.com/ Home Services
   https://www.housecallpro.com/ Home Services
   https://lawyerist.com/ Legal
   https://www.topproducer.com/ Realtors
   https://chirofusionsoftware.com/ Chiropractors
   https://www.mountstride.com/ Dental
   https://www.dentalcrm.com/ Dental
   https://www.gymmaster.com/ Fitness
   https://pos.toasttab.com/ Restaurants
   https://www.getcanopy.com/Accounting Firms
   https://www.ezyvet.com/ Veterinarian

7. **Database marketing software:** This systematically helps you set up and run email marketing campaigns for cold prospects, warm leads, current clients, and past clients.

   https://www.activecampaign.com/
   https://mailchimp.com/
   https://www.constantcontact.com/

https://www.sendinblue.com/

https://www.aweber.com/

8. **Funnel and automation software:** This allows you to systematically tag each lead and set up specific logic tables (funnels). The software moves them to the next step based off their actions (or non-actions). It's as simple as, "If this happens, then do this, if that happens, then do this instead." You can get as complicated as you want.

https://clickfunnels.com/

https://gohighlevel.com/

https://kartra.com/

https://kajabi.com/

https://funnelpages.com/

https://keap.com/

https://ontraport.com/

9. **Chatbot:** This is an app that automatically interacts with your online traffic. This could be on Facebook or your website. The bot, similar to other funnel software, pushes your leads through logic tables, quickly segmenting them based off their interactions and answers.

https://wordpress.org/plugins/wp-chatbot/

https://manychat.com/

https://www.zendesk.com/service/answer-bot/

https://continual.ly/

https://birdeye.com/

10. **Team chat software:**

https://slack.com For a chat-powered workplace.

https://www.microsoft.com/en-us/microsoft-teams/group-chat-software for large organizations broken down into teams.

https://workspace.google.com/products/chat/ for Google Workspace (formerly G Suite) users.

https://mattermost.com/ for self-hosted team chat.

11. **Online appointment scheduling software:**

https://calendly.com/

https://acuityscheduling.com/

https://getjobber.com/ For home services

12. **Connection software:** This quickly and easily allows you to connect to different software and have them communicate with each other. It's a must-have for complicated funnels that intertwine your email software with your CRM, with your Google Ads, and Facebook Ads, and so on.

http://zapier.com/

13. **Miscellaneous tools:**

Video Speed Controller: (Chrome extension) Speed up, slow down, advance and rewind HTML5 audio/video with shortcuts. This can save you oodles of time watching videos on YouTube or Facebook. I watch most everything at 1.3 speed effectively saving me a third of the time.

Keywords Everywhere Tool: (Chrome Extension) Shows keyword search volume, cost-per-click averages, and competition for websites like Google Search Console, YouTube, Amazon, and more.

Bitwarden: Free secure password manager for all your devices.

Awesome Screenshot & Screen Recorder: Free screen capture and annotation tool. Easily clip images or record your screen. Definitely comes in handy, I use it at least a dozen times a day.

CHAPTER 5

GET OFF YOUR ASSET
(Actions, Execution, Productivity)

Action is the foundational key to all success.
—*Pablo Picasso*

30K FOOT VIEW

The quote above is appropriate for this chapter because, although Picasso is known for his amazing talents, it is his actions that truly made him world class and in a league of his own. Picasso was exceptionally prolific throughout his long lifetime. It is verifiably true that he produced over 50,000 unique pieces of art in various media. His oeuvre was ultimately left to his heirs and comprised 13,500 paintings, 1,228 sculptures, 2,880 ceramics, roughly 12,000 drawings, many thousands of prints and engravings, and numerous tapestries and rugs. Just to put that into perspective, he started his professional career at age 15 and made his last painting at 91 years old. That's over 76 years of creating art, which averages 658 pieces a year, or almost two a day, consistently. Most of us don't even brush our teeth twice a day consistently.

Pablo truly was a man of action, which was the key to his success and is the key to your success.

In the book *Art & Fear*, authors David Bayles and Ted Orland share a similar factual story about a ceramics teacher. Here's what transpired:

The ceramics teacher announced that he was dividing the class into two groups. All those on the left side of the studio, he said, would be graded solely on the quantity of work they produced, and all those on the right solely on its quality.

His procedure was simple: on the final day of class, he would bring in his bathroom scales and weigh the work of the "quantity" group: fifty pounds of pots rated an "A," forty pounds a "B," and so on. Those being graded on "quality," however, needed to produce only one pot—albeit a perfect one—to get an "A."

Well, grading time came, and a curious fact emerged: the works of highest quality were all produced by the group being graded for quantity!

It seems that while the "quantity" group was busily churning out piles of work—and learning from their mistakes—the "quality" group had sat around theorizing about perfection, and in the end had little more to show for their efforts than grandiose theories and a pile of dead clay.

This story establishes Picasso's statement in that action is the foundational key to all success.

There are probably hundreds of stories of success from people who take consistent action. One of my favorites is Jerry Seinfeld. When he was younger, he knew the best way to write better jokes was to write a lot of jokes and be consistent. So, Jerry went out and got a wall calendar, and when he wrote a joke on the first day, he put an X on that date. The next day he wrote a joke, then he put an X on that date. Before long he had a chain of Xs. His only job then was to not break the chain. He would file his jokes in a little accordion folder and sometimes he would bring that folder on stage and pull out a joke. It wasn't long before he became one of the greatest comedians of all time.

Another success story with someone who takes consistent action is author and leadership coach John Maxwell. He claims that his success is simply from doing five things every day. He calls it his rule of five. For John, his rule of five is as follows: every day he reads, every day he files, every day he thinks, every day he asks questions, and every day he writes. You may ask, What about Christmas? John would say, "Every day." What about your birthday? "Every day." What about when you are on an Alaskan cruise with your wife? "EVERY DAY." There is no question why John Maxwell is the greatest leadership author and coach of all time.

The pinnacle question is how do you, specifically YOU, change your behaviors and start taking consistent positive actions? Obviously, it's easier said than done. There is an excellent aphorism attributed to Dr. Henry Cloud and Dr. John Townsend that says, "Until the pain of staying the same is worse than the pain of change, people won't change. It is consequences that give us the pain that motivates us to change."

Unfortunately, most people don't want to change their behavior; they want to change the consequences of their behavior.

Most consequences are not enough to get someone to change and take a new action; they would rather keep the pain of staying the same. Even people in dire situations have only a 10 percent chance they'll actually change for good.

As we learned earlier from Newton, it's easy to understand the physics that an object at rest tends to stay at rest unless acted upon. The answer to how to overcome complacency is to act or be acted upon.

IN THE TRENCHES

Psychologists proclaim the two best ways to change deep-seated behavior and take new positive actions are "shaping" and "immersion."

Shaping

Shaping is slow, methodical, successive approximations that progressively move you toward the desired results. It's a series of rewards that provide positive reinforcement for behavior changes that are successive steps toward the final desired behavior. Using micro quotas to reach macro goals is an excellent way to form new positive behavioral habits, and start and continue taking actions.

Shaping has been around for multi-millennia, probably since Adam and Eve were instructed to "dress and keep" the garden of Eden. However, shaping wasn't truly recognized in psychology until B. F. Skinner "shaped" pigeons to bowl. Yes, you read that right. One of the greatest psychologists of the century was fooling around and taught pigeons to bowl. Skinner later wrote an article in *American Psychologist* and described the observation. He wrote:

> In 1943, Keller Breland, Norman Guttman, and I were working on a war-time project sponsored by General Mills, Inc. Our laboratory was the top floor of a flour mill in Minneapolis, where we spent a good deal of time waiting for decisions to be made in Washington. All day long, around the mill, wheeled great flocks of pigeons. They were easily snared on the windowsills and proved to be an irresistible supply of experimental subjects. This was serious research, but we had our lighter moments. One day we decided to teach a pigeon to bowl. The pigeon was to send a wooden ball down a miniature alley toward a set of toy pins by swiping the ball with a sharp sideward movement of the beak. To condition the response, we put the ball on the floor of an experimental box and prepared to operate the food-magazine as soon as the first swipe occurred. But nothing happened. Though we had all the time in the world, we grew tired of waiting. We decided to reinforce any response which had the slightest resemblance to a swipe—perhaps, at first, merely the behavior of looking at the ball—and then to select responses which more closely approximated the final form. The result

amazed us. In a few minutes, the ball was caroming off the walls of the box as if the pigeon had been a champion squash player. (Skinner, *American Psychologist*, 1958, p. 94)

A modern example of shaping in today's world is participation trophies. Trust me, I know how controversial this subject is because my wife and I own a trophy shop and I teach recognition and engagement programs all over the United States. Here's how participation trophies actually should work in the real world to "shape" our children. Coaches of very young athletic teams will usually buy a trophy for every player who played the entire season. They showed up for practice and played in the games and ultimately got better. Anyone who has coached a T-ball team knows there is a drastic difference in participation by the end of the season. At first, they may have run the wrong way on the bases or were mostly drawing in the dirt, but by the last game, they were present and trying, they voluntarily participated, thus the name.

The coach rewards and recognizes them with a sparkling trophy with their name on it, which is a powerful reinforcement for positive behaviors. This starts shaping their little impressionable brains and introduces them to exceptional virtues like stick-to-itiveness, teamwork, competition, humility, patience, and a host of other useful skills they may have not yet learned, and its effects can last a lifetime. This is equivalent to giving a puppy a treat to sit. At first, you may have to push her butt down to the sit position, then give her the reward. Then you say "Sit," and you reward her for moving like she was going to sit. Then when she actually sits, you reward her hugely. Your puppy will quickly learn what the word "sit" means and do it on command.

Just like your puppy, you at first reward children for simple elementary tasks until they "get it." And just like Skinner's experiment, there is a point at which you no longer reward for just moving toward the action you want them to take. You don't continue to give the pigeon food just because he turned toward the ball, and you certainly don't give participation trophies to little leaguers. You only reward for victory. It's a succession of shaping that propels animals, children, and adults to push beyond their current abilities.

Another example of shaping is if you want to run a 5K, you would first start with just buying some new running shoes and workout clothes. Then the next day, you just put them on. Then the next day, maybe you put your workout clothes on, walk outside, and stretch for 10 minutes. Then the next day, maybe you walk around the block. Then the next day, you run half the block and walk half the block, and so on. Within a couple weeks, if you are consistent and take successive steps toward your goal, you should be able to easily run 5K. Obviously, this is way oversimplified, but it absolutely does work with animals and humans.

Immersion

There's just one way to radically change your behavior:
radically change your environment.
—*Dr. B. J. Fogg*

Another excellent way to change deep-seated behavior is immersion. This is where you jump in with both feet, where you are completely engulfed, engrossed, absorbed in a new environment, leaving you no way to go back to the old habits. Drug and alcohol rehab centers, marriage retreats, cultural exchange students, fat farms, and prisons are all immersion conversion programs, and they work extremely well.

Many bestselling authors immerse themselves in their writing by renting a cabin in the woods with no distractions. Many Olympic athletes move to other countries to prepare for the games. Even Rocky moved to Russia to train in the elements for the fight of his life. In all seriousness, many actors immerse themselves into a role before acting in a movie. This is called "method" acting. Heath Ledger locked himself in a London motel for 43 days, scribbling out daily diary entries as the caped crusader's arch-nemesis, to prepare for his role as the Joker. Val Kilmer's epic portrayal of Jim Morrison in *The Doors* is the stuff of legends. To begin with, the actor learned how to play and sing about fifty of his songs, and lived for a year as the indelible Morrison, dressing in his clothes and embodying the singer's awkward and strange movements. The immersion apparently paid off; after listening to recordings from the movie, actual members of the band were unable to tell the difference between Kilmer's performance and Morrison's. After production, Kilmer went into therapy to "get out" of character because he was so completely immersed.

If you want to drastically change your life, you must change your environment. If you want to become a better person, you must surround yourself with people who embody the traits you want to develop and disassociate with the ones who don't. If you want to be a healthier person, you must make healthy choices the easiest option, by clearing your cupboards and fridge of all the junk food. If you want to be more productive, you must place yourself in a situation where productivity is the path of least resistance.

Partial immersion is certainly an option, though it's nowhere near as powerful as full immersion. Partial immersion could be non-negotiable weekly or monthly meetings with a mastermind or coach. This will definitely get you to take action.

Other partial immersion tactics could be time-blocking several hours a day or week to work on something specific in your business. Close your door, shut off all distractions like your phone and email, and immerse yourself in your project for the allotted time.

One of my favorite partial immersion tactics are online masterclasses or challenges. This is where you immerse yourself in a live online training for a specified number of days. Each day the guru gives you homework assignments that must be completed by the next day. Challenges are terrific for stimulating new behaviors because of two things: they have deadlines and they have a built-in herd community. Everyone is doing things way out of their comfort zone and posting videos about it. All the participants encourage everyone else to take action and move ahead. The moderators immediately ban and delete any negative comments, and what's left is a wall of cheerleaders. It's truly an amazing and dynamic environment. Statistically there is an unusual amount of success that comes from these live online interactive trainings.

I need to wrap up this chapter on action by specifically defining what is real action.

I'm a huge believer in setting daily "tactical" goals: something you can actually check off a list. For instance, I set a goal to work out 208 times a year. This equates to four days a week on average. I don't set a goal to lose weight and get into better shape, even though I undoubtably will, but those are not tactics I can check off. You need to be extremely specific in your daily or weekly tactics. I further define "working out" as a two-plus mile run, 30 minutes of heavy weight training, or twelve thousand steps in a day. At the end of the day, it's a simple yes or no on the question: "Did I work out?" You should do the same in setting your yearly goals by breaking them down into daily and weekly tactical achievements that you can check off a calendar. If you want to sell more in your business, you could set the weekday tactical goal of five in-person cold calls a day or ten cold outreach phone calls a day or two hundred cold outreach emails a day. These are called "lead indicators," and it's the easiest metric to track the actions that will ultimately lead to more sales.

Once you define how many cold outreaches it takes to make an appointment, then you can find out how many appointments it takes to make a sale (appointments are also "lead indicators"). Your focus is on the daily activity that, if done consistently, will absolutely make you successful. By using the tactical, goal planning strategy, there are only two ways you can fail. 1.) You set up the wrong daily tactics. 2.) You did not execute; you did not do the daily activity that produces a result. This makes it quite easy to troubleshoot what went wrong.

Picasso is absolutely right in that action is the foundational key to all success, and it's most definitely the key to your success. It's not intellect we lack but emotional determination and strength to act. Remember, you have been given four amazing, unique human endowments by your creator. Let us not squander them and succumb to mediocrity, or worse, failure. At the end of our lives, it is assured that we will be more disappointed by the things we did not do than by the things we did do. Resolve to stop wishing, stop "shoulding" all over yourself, and plan specifically what you will do each day to propel you and your business forward, and then resolve to work your plan consistently. Ignite strong feelings. Get mad! Indifference is a disease that causes stagnation. Disgust and resolve are two powerful emotions that will help you act. Disgust says that "you have had it." Resolve says, "I will." Action puts fear to flight. No excuses, just action. Mark the X on your calendar and keep the chain going.

Today is just tomorrow's yesterday. What are you going to do today that makes a difference in your life? What's the one thing you can do today to move you toward your goals? What one action can you take today that if you do it consistently and do it well, will propel your business forward? Whatever your answer is, do it today! The new you starts right now.

I will finish this chapter with my all-time favorite quotes about taking actions. Don't skip over these. Read them, and they will inspire you to take action!

The path to success is to take massive, determined actions.
——Anthony Robbins

Do you want to know who you are? Don't ask. Act!
Action will delineate and define you.
——Thomas Jefferson

You don't have to be great to start, but you have to start to be great.
——Joe Sabah

Inaction breeds doubt and fear. Action
breeds confidence and courage.
If you want to conquer fear, do not sit home and think about it.
Go out and get busy.
——Dale Carnegie

Movement is a medicine for creating change in a person's physical, emotional, and mental states.
—Carol Welch

An idea not coupled with action will never get any bigger than the brain cell it occupied.
—Arnold Glasow

Well done is better than well said.
—Benjamin Franklin

Dost thou love life? Then do not squander time, for that is the stuff life is made of.
—Benjamin Franklin

Action is a great restorer and builder of confidence. Inaction is not only the result, but the cause, of fear.
—Norman Vincent Peale

Take the first step in faith. You don't have to see the whole staircase, just take the first step.
—Dr. Martin Luther King, Jr.

Things may come to those who wait, but only the things left by those who hustle.
—Abraham Lincoln

The universe doesn't give you what you want in your mind; it gives you what you demand with your actions.
—Steve Maraboli

The best way to get started is to quit talking and begin doing.
——Walt Disney

Small deeds done are better than great deeds planned.
——Peter Marshall

Vision without action is daydream. Action
without vision is nightmare.
——Japanese proverb

The word is ACT. Because far too often, I've
allowed good thoughts and good words and good
intentions to stop short of good actions.
——Author unknown

"How foolish! Can't you see that faith without good deeds is
useless? Don't you remember that our ancestor Abraham was
shown to be right with God by his actions when he offered
his son Isaac on the altar? You see, his faith and his actions
worked together. His actions made his faith complete. And so,
it happened just as the Scriptures say: 'Abraham believed God,
and God counted him as righteous because of his faith.' He
was even called the friend of God. So, you see, we are shown
to be right with God by what we do, not by faith alone. Rahab
the prostitute is another example. She was shown to be right
with God by her actions when she hid those messengers and sent
them safely away by a different road. Just as the body is dead
without breath, so also faith is dead without good works."
——James 2:20–26

SECTION 2

CHAPTER 6

KLTTBE
(Customer Journey)

All things being equal, people will do business with—
and refer business to—
those people they know, like, and trust.
—Bob Burg

People do business with people they know, like, and trust.

First off, it says "People do business with people." Every single one of us does business with living, breathing human beings. Not "the Machine," not "Corporate," not "the Organization," not "the System," not "the Firm," not "the Party," not "the Institution," not "the Establishment," not "the Agency," and not robots (not yet, anyway). We do business with people. This is extremely important to remember and keep at the forefront of our minds. Even trillion-dollar corporations are run by individual people. If you want to do business with that corporation, you must contact, schedule an appointment with, pitch, negotiate, and persuade a person or persons. I think we sometimes forget that on the other end of the phone, voicemail, email, or Zoom call is a real human being. A person who puts their pants on one leg at a time and more than likely has emotions, issues, and problems like the rest of us. Along the same lines, if you own a small to medium business (SMB), you are personally, unequivocally associated with your business, and it's almost impossible to disassociate yourself. Business is not just business for a small business owner; it's personal and your business is unambiguously tied to you personally whether you like it or not.

People do business with people they know, like, and trust. That's the first part of the customer journey. The entire journey is the acronym KLTTBE. It stands for **K**now, **L**ike, **T**rust, **T**ry, **B**uy, **E**vangelize. This is the exact path—the journey you must take with your customers. First you must get them to know you and your company. Then you must get them to like you and trust you. Once that is established, the customer will "try" you and your services or product. They will dip their toe in the water and hesitantly and cautiously make a transaction with your business. If they have a pleasant experience, the customer will then "buy" you. They will shift all the business they can to you and buy from you repeatedly. Then they will evangelize for you. They'll tell all their friends and family to use you and give you glowing testimonials.

Now that you understand the journey, you can strategically and purposefully help move customers along each step of that path.

CHAPTER 7

KNOW
(Circle of Influence)

*If you want to upgrade your circle of influ-
ence, it begins with upgrading yourself.*
—Hal Elrod

30K FOOT VIEW

To know you and your business means an awareness in the minds of consumers from experience, observation, or rumor. People who "know" you and your business bring about a memory when triggered with your name or logo. Those memories that are recalled is your brand. Another word for "know" is "brand." A brand is simply the sum total of all mental associations (good and bad) that are triggered with a name or logo. A brand is a person's perception of a person, product, service, experience, or organization. Marty Neumeier, author and speaker on all things brand, defines *brand* in his book *The Brand Gap* by first laying out what a brand is not: "A brand is not a logo. A brand is not an identity. A brand is not a product." Neumeier goes on to say that "A brand is a person's gut feeling about a product, service, or organization."

Personal branding expert Gary Vaynerchuk explains brand as reputation. Gary Vee has been known to say that whenever you hear the word brand, just think of "reputation." They mean the same thing! A brand is not what the business says it is; a brand is what customers tell their friends it is.

For instance, if I said "Apple," your mind would immediately recall your experiences with that brand, and you can easily pick different adjectives to describe it. Some of you would say innovative, ingenuity, trendy, hip, user-friendly, secure, you may even say the word "revolutionary." Others may say extortionate, sheeple, restrictive, cultic, overrated. These are all words that are associated with that brand. Some of the words were formed from repetitious marketing, others from user experience, others from observation, and others from hearsay.

What does your business name or logo stimulate in the mind of consumers? Obviously, these perceptions happen naturally, but we want to control or at least influence the words associated with our business. So how do we do that?

IN THE TRENCHES
Two Ways to Get More People to Know You and Your Business

There are only two ways to get more people to know your business or your brand and you must do both.

1. Word of mouth
2. Marketing

Word of Mouth

Remember the last time you experienced something, and you just had to tell your friends about it? It might have been a new movie, a new restaurant, a shop that just opened, or the latest gadget you're infatuated with. Whether you are talking or posting a reel about it, this excitement to share is what drives word of mouth. On the contrary, the same word of mouth happens with negative experiences. In general, negative experiences spread three times faster and further than positive experiences. Knowing this, what do we do about it? The answer is we must strategically and purposefully control it and then propagate the positive word of mouth.

One of the best strategic word-of-mouth stories is from Zappos. If you go to Zappos' frequently asked questions, you will see this: "Q: I want to return my purchase! What do I do? A: If you are not 100% satisfied with your purchase from Zappos, you can return your item(s) for a full refund within 365 days of purchase."

Then in 2012, Matt Burchard, Sr., director of marketing for Zappos.com, sent out a brilliant press release that said that leap year customers should not be penalized just because the month of February will only have 28 days next year. "As an organization focused on customer service, our number one goal at Zappos is to make people happy," said Burchard. "Giving our leap year customers 1,461 days to return, or more simply put, four years, seemed like a wonderful way to celebrate Leap Year."

Unfortunately, when I ask local brick-and-mortar businesses how they perpetuate positive word of mouth, their answer is usually, "We have great customer service." "Do you really?" I ask. If your customer service experience isn't as outrageous as Zappos,' then no one is talking about it. But why can't it be?

In my town, we have a remarkable, extraordinarily successful (allegedly bringing in over $22 million a year from one location), local, private restaurant that is genuinely world famous for at least eight absurd reasons. Each of these items were created on purpose to promote their brand through word of mouth. Here are the eight absurd things.

1. There are over 1.5 million $1 bills stapled to the ceiling. No, I have not counted them, but I'll take their word for it. If you saw it, you would believe it too. It started with a $1 tip that the owner, Molly Martin, stapled to the bar over 40 years ago. People started following suit, and today it's one of the most preposterous things

you will ever see. My problem is that money is inherently very dirty, and I don't want a bunch of it hovering over my steak. So, I asked the manager about it, and he said they have all the money professionally cleaned and sanitized at least once per year. Good answer.

2.   One of their appetizers is "Senate Bean Soup," which costs a ridiculous 18 cents. The story goes that the soup is the same recipe that was once served in the United States Senate. In the 1920s, an Irish immigrant from County Clare named Padraig McGraith was employed in the U.S. Senate cafeteria as a dishwasher. Washington, D.C., was a long way from the Emerald Isle, and Padraig missed the hearty soups and stews of home. He also had 11 children and needed to stretch his grocery budget as much as possible. The chefs in the Senate kitchen would listen to Paddy's homesick laments and finally decided to ask him how to make an authentic and hearty soup. Paddy assembled the ingredients from what was at hand. Paddy was so sure that the head chef would love his soup that he bet a day's pay it would be a hit, and of course it was. Paddy made 18 cents a day at the time, and the cost of the soup has never gone up since 1977. The restaurant menu flippantly says, "The Senate cafeteria has raised their price to $7.00, but we all know Washington can't control costs."

3.   This privately owned restaurant has won hundreds of local, regional, and national awards for their food. They have an amazing, diverse menu with delectable meals fit for a king. Their slogan is "Feasting, Imbibing, and Debauchery." One of their absurdities that promotes positive word of mouth is the size of their meal portions. My favorite sandwich is affectionately called the "Mile-High Reuben." I didn't use a micrometer, but the corned beef, sauerkraut, and cheese was stacked over four inches high (not including the bread). Over 75 percent of their customers use a

to-go box (I'm sorry to reveal I finished mine). The owner was quoted, saying, "I don't want anyone leaving hungry."

4. If you look closely at the menu, you will find a $100 hamburger. I've never indulged in one myself, but I hear it is a phenomenal hamburger. The restaurant takes a filet mignon, turns it into a patty, and serves it with a side of caviar and a bottle of Moët Imperial champagne. Surprisingly, they sell a few almost every day.

5. Speaking of burgers, their normal hamburgers are premium Angus steak burgers, custom ground by their own butchers from their steak trimmings. The patties are a massive three-quarter pound of lean beef with a blend of seasonings rubbed into handmade steak burgers. I tell you all this because they have what's called the "Alka-Seltzer Award." If you tell them in advance, you can eat three burgers, succeed, and they'll award you a free T-shirt and an Alka-Seltzer. (Of course, you must pay for all three burgers.)

6. We covered the "feasting" part in numbers three through five, but just as important to their brand is the "Imbibing and Debauchery." Their wine cellar holds 8,000 bottles of wine, some of which are 20 grand a bottle. Their magnificent wine list is the winner of *Wine Spectator Magazine*'s Best of Award of Excellence. This restaurant has also won dozens of awards for its state-of-the-art microbrewery. One of the smartest things they do is sell you a membership into the "Mug Club." This is where you purchase a ceramic beer stein for $26.99, and they will personalize it with your name and customer number on it, and whatever clever saying you want. These mugs are stored on the ceiling by number all throughout the restaurant. The "Mug Club" entitles you to get $2 draft beers and $2.50 well drinks on Wednesdays.

7. The pub has amazing live music, including the world-famous Irish Pub Pipe Band that serenades you with bagpipes and drums. Other regional Irish musicians play almost every weekend. The absurd thing is, if you want to make a request, you must kiss the moose

(pre-COVID). Yes, they have a real moose head on the wall that you must actually kiss to get your song played. It would be terrifying to swab culture its lips.

8. This last one is by far my favorite word-of-mouth absurdity at the restaurant. When you go to the bathrooms, there is a huge sign on the door with large bold letters that says "Men's," then on the side of the sign, it says "This way men" with an inconspicuous arrow pointing to the next door over. And on the women's door, it's vice versa. The look on people's faces when they come running back out after they realize they are in the wrong bathroom is absolutely hysterical. Unfortunately, a few years back someone reported it to the Department of Business and Professional Regulation, which ordered the restaurant to change the signage. This quickly became national news covered by the Associated Press. The restaurant got over 3,000 patrons to sign a petition to keep the signage. Eventually they came to an agreement that would allow the restaurant to keep their famous signs posted; but installed a second set of swinging doors after the signs but before the restroom areas. All of this was a huge positive word of mouth for the restaurant.

Now that you know these eight things about the restaurant, what is the chance you would visit it if you were to visit my town? (By the way, I'd love to meet you there if you are in town. I'll buy the bean soup.)

I'm not saying your business has to be as absurd as this restaurant. But I am saying there is always something you can do to create some positive local buzz. Word of mouth is an excellent way to get more prospects to "know" you and your business.

Marketing

The second way to get more people to "know" you and your business is by marketing. According to the American Marketing Association (AMA), marketing can be defined as "the activity, set of institutions, and processes for creating, communicating, delivering, and exchanging offerings that have value for customers, clients, partners, and society at large." So, by definition, marketing includes all advertising, and your business cards, your storefront location(s), your vehicles, and anything else that would represent your business.

There is little agreement about when marketing first began. Some researchers claim that marketing tactics can be found in antiquity while others suggest that marketing, in its modern form, developed in conjunction with the rise of consumer culture in the seventeenth and eighteenth century, while yet other researchers propose that modern marketing was only fully realized in the decades following the Industrial Revolution.

The *Oxford English Dictionary* traces the abstract usage of the word "marketing" only as far back as 1884.

For the purposes of this book, I am only referencing the modern form of marketing, which has a single purpose of persuading people to use your business. This type of marketing is, in fact, somewhat of a recent development.

After World War II, goods and service producers were generally scarce and business owners could sell pretty much all that they could produce, if people could afford to buy them. There wasn't much need for marketing, advertising, and branding until local competition and capitalism grew. It was at that point when communication and persuading potential customers that one manufacturer's goods were better than another became vital to a business's success. Having a choice on which business to use forced business owners to step up their game.

By the 1960s, almost all niches had become completely saturated locally, regionally, and nationally; however, the size of their respective markets has remained relatively the same. Fortunately for consumers but unfortunately for business owners, from here on out, there will always be intense competition for customers, and some form of marketing is mandatory for lasting success.

Marketing is an excellent way to get more people to know you and your business. It's controllable, scalable, and once dialed in, somewhat predictable. The downside is most small business owners are partly to mostly clueless on how to achieve a ROI (return on investment) on their marketing efforts. The majority throw money haphazardly to the usual marketing channels and pray for the best. Less than 30 percent of small and medium businesses (SMBs) actually track the efficacy of their marketing.

John Wanamaker (1838–1922) was a remarkably successful business owner, religious leader, and political figure, considered by some to be a "pioneer in marketing." He opened one of the first and most successful department stores in the United States, which grew to 16 stores and eventually became part of Macy's. Wanamaker invented the price tag. Before him, most buying was done by haggling. A devout Christian, he believed that if everyone was equal before God, then everyone should be equal before price. Wanamaker is also credited with coining the phrase "Half the money I spend on advertising is wasted; the trouble is, I don't know which half." That statement makes sense for 1922, but there is no reason to not know your results in today's digital world. I cannot use the word "definitive" quite yet, but it's close. Certainly, you should have a fairly accurate idea that if you spent $1 on advertising and got back $1.10 or $2 or $10 or 90 cents.

One of the tools I listed earlier is dynamic call tracking. Because I own a call tracking company, I have the fortune to see amazing analytic data from hundreds of thousands of inbound calls that come from dozens of different online and offline marketing sources. Each call is tracked, recorded, and labeled with the outcome. You don't have to guess which marketing channels work anymore.

For the sake of clarity and simplicity, I'm going to break down marketing into two types: 1.) Brand awareness marketing 2.) Direct response marketing. Both are excellent ways to get more prospects to "know" you. Also, there are only two types of prospects: 1.) Business to Business (B2B) 2.) Business to Consumer (B2C).

It's beyond the scope of this book to get into the complete tactical details of "how to do" these types of marketing, but I do want to cover some of the basics and the "why."

Brand Awareness Marketing

I briefly discussed the definition of a brand in the beginning of this chapter. The branding experts say that all brands can be placed in one or more of these three categories.

1. Corporate brand
2. Product/service brand
3. Personal brand

Corporate brands tend to have many different product brands under the same umbrella, like Disney, Chevrolet, Apple, Nike, and so forth.

Product brands may have a corporate identity attached to them, like a Ford Mustang or McDonald's Big Mac. Some product brands just stand on their own, like Red Bull.

Personal brands are attached to a single person like Anthony Robbins or Kevin Hart, or they can be a small group like the Beatles or the Blue Man Group.

The "Pros" of Brand Awareness Marketing

1. If you stop advertising, your brand will continue to live on and serve you for quite a while. It is possible to hit "critical mass" with branding where your brand is so powerful that it will last for generations.
2. If consumers have to make a choice, they will ultimately choose the brand they are most familiar with and the brand they feel most comfortable with.

The "Cons" of Brand Awareness Marketing

1. It's a long-term building process, even with a big budget. If your brand is misaligned or incongruent, branding may actually backfire on you.

2. It's a never-ending process. Except for those few that broke through critical mass, you will always have to keep paying for branding marketing. One of the main reasons is that because of market turnover, you will never "arrive," and thus you must continue to build your brand, or you will eventually slide backward.

3. It's harder to quantify results and thus could be an expense and not necessarily an investment.

Even with these issues, I still strongly believe that all local SMBs (especially you and your business), should be marketing your corporate brand and your personal brand combined. If you own a plumbing company or an accounting firm or a dental practice in average town America, your local market should absolutely know your company name, as well as you, the business owner.

Direct Response Marketing

The second type of marketing for SMBs is direct response marketing, which is exactly as it sounds. It's an advertisement that requests a specific action. It could be directing prospects to go to this location, go to this website, fill in a form, call this number, text this number, use this code, and so on.

The "Pros" of Direct Response Marketing

1. **You will get immediate feedback on whether or not your marketing is converting.**

2. You can split test each ad to see which one gets better results.

3. It's easily quantifiable and trackable and should give you a return on your investment (ROI).

4. With enough frequency or a good enough offer, it can overcome a strong competitor's brand.

The "Cons" of Direct Response Marketing

1. If you stop advertising, you stop getting results immediately.
2. It can take a while to dial in before getting respectable results.
3. Your ads must talk directly to your prospect to get their attention. In addition, your ad copy must be persuasive enough to get them to take the action you want them to take.

I am strongly advocating that SMBs strategically do both brand awareness and direct response marketing on a local level. Direct response works vastly better with a solidified brand. And brand awareness alone is hard to scale.

People do business with people they know, like, and trust. Step one is to grow your circle of influence in your market and get more people to "know" you and your business. One of your main jobs as a business owner is to grow your circle of influence strategically, systematically, and consistently. This does not happen by accident. Marketing must be a part of your business plan. In my marketing agency, we sell packages that coincide with the "Know," "Like," and "Trust" marketing model. In our "Know" packages, we specifically work on direct response and brand marketing that will dramatically and methodically grow their circle of influence. We focus primarily on digital marketing, so I will quickly go through the best way to get more prospects to "know" you, which is to grow your circle of influence with online marketing.

Google Business Profile (GBP)

The foundation and absolute undisputed best marketing to get inbound leads for all local, brick-and-mortar businesses, (SMBs) is your Google Business Profile (GBP), which is your listing on Google Maps. New businesses are the exception because they have no brand recognition yet nor would they rank anywhere on the maps. Let me say that again to make sure you grasp the importance of this. If you are a local SMB who sells to local patrons, the number one way to get leads or customers is by far your GBP listing!

We discussed your GBP profile listing earlier in Chapter 4, "Toolset." I stressed how critically important your listing is for your business. For almost all of our established clients that my agency works with, Google Maps is credited for over half of all inbound calls, for some of our clients, it's over 75 percent of their leads. It's astonishing to see the power of something that Google gives you for free. Google Maps is simply a directory, similar to Yellow Pages a generation ago, but the GBP listings are ranked in order of authority, not alphabetical. Fortunately, that's why no new companies are named "AAA Plumbing" or "Aardvark Landscaping." On a side note, early in my marketing career, I remember asking why they chose that particular name for their business, and they said, "To be first in the phone book." My only thought was if that's your marketing plan, you are in trouble. (No offense to all the AAA and Aardvark business owners reading this book.)

Are you tracking your calls, leads, form fills, direction requests? If you are, you would know I'm correct. Think about it: if you need your carpets cleaned, you simply Google the brand name of the company you know, like, and trust then you call them from the phone number on Google Maps. Or, if you have no loyalties to a company, you Google "carpet cleaning companies near me," look at the maps listings, and pick one to call. Statistics show that about 65 to 75 percent will do a little research and look at their website, but in the end, they are going to call one of them. All marketing experts agree that this is the new norm, and there is not an alternative anywhere in sight.

So, just to solidify my position on this, it's absolutely essential that you have a plan to increase your online authority and make sure you are capitalizing on the best form of free marketing on earth. Search engine optimization (SEO), which includes optimizing your Google Business Profile listing, is still enormously important, especially on a local level. I passionately recommend you take a class on how to grow your online authority or hire a digital marketing agency to do it for you. Your GBP will serve you for many years to come and is a terrific way to get new people to "know" your business.

Google Ads

Another excellent way to get people to know your business is by "paid" online marketing. Google Ads is a powerful way to get new people to find your business through search. With Google Ads, (formerly known as AdWords), you can bid on keywords that are relevant to your business. If someone types in "AC repair company" and you own a HVAC company, wouldn't you want to talk with that person? There is not a hotter lead than someone searching for exactly what you do. That's the awesomeness of Google Ads. If you are not ranking in maps for those keywords, you can use Google Ads and bid to have your ad at the top when someone searches it. It may take three to seven clicks on average before you get a true lead, but it will absolutely get you new business that would have never found you otherwise.

Local Services Ads (LSA)

Similar to Google Ads is Local Services Ads (LSA), or sometimes called Google Guaranteed ads, because Google actually guarantees your service. If a customer is unhappy with the quality of your work, Google may refund up to the amount paid for jobs booked through Local Services Ads, with a lifetime cap for coverage. Because Google is backing you and your company, you must first be vetted. Google hires a third party to run background checks on the owners and all your employees, your location, phone number, licenses, and insurance to get your business verified. I heard rumors that they do anal cavity checks, but I cannot verify that.

Once you are finally approved, Google will serve up your ad at the very top of the search results with two other Google Guaranteed competitors based off the following criteria.

- Your weekly budget
- Your proximity to potential customers' location
- Your review score and the number of reviews you receive
- Your responsiveness to customer inquiries and requests
- Your business hours
- Whether or not they have received serious or repeated complaints about your business

The best part about LSA is you only pay for booked appointments. All the calls are recorded by Google, and you can tag them as booked or not. If they aren't relevant or are not a legitimate lead, you can dispute the lead and Google won't charge you. So, the cost for a booked appointment is usually dramatically cheaper than PPC. With traditional text ads, you will pay for an average of three to seven clicks before you actually get a true lead (depending on your niche, market, and competition).

Unfortunately, Local Services Ads are limited to certain local service companies. They are adding more niches in more markets, but as of now, here is the list.

- Appliance repair services
- Architecture services
- Carpenters
- Carpet cleaning services
- Cleaning services

- Countertop services
- Electricians
- Event planning services
- Fencing services
- Financial planning services
- Flooring services
- Foundations services
- Garage door services
- HVAC (heating or air conditioning)
- Interior designers
- Junk removal services
- Landscaping services
- Lawn care services
- Lawyers
    - Bankruptcy lawyer services
    - Business lawyer services
    - Contract lawyer services
    - Criminal lawyer services
    - Disability lawyer services
    - DUI (Driving Under the Influence) lawyer services
    - Estate lawyer services
    - Family lawyer services
    - Immigration lawyer services
    - IP lawyer services
    - Labor lawyer services
    - Litigation lawyer services
    - Malpractice lawyer services
    - Personal injury lawyer services
    - Real estate lawyer
    - Real estate services
    - Traffic lawyer services

- Locksmiths
- Movers
- Pest control services
- Photographers
- Plumbers
- Real estate services
- Realtors
- Roofers
- Siding services
- Tax services
- Tree services
- Videographers
- Water damage services
- Window cleaning services
- Window repair services

If your niche is on that list, I strongly recommend you go through the pain of getting set up for LSA. As of this writing, except for your GBP, there is not a cheaper way of getting new business online. As more competitors sign up, the cost will go up.

I'll wrap up this chapter with a few other great ways to grow your circle of influence and get more people to know you and your business.

Intrusive Marketing

Intrusive marketing, sometimes called interruption marketing, is where you push an advertisement in front of perspective customers. This could be in the form of traditional media like billboards, radio, TV, direct mail, urinal signs, and so on. Intrusive ads online can be shown on all social media platforms like Facebook, Instagram, Twitter, TikTok, and so forth. Other great intrusive marketing can be display ads on ad networks that will show your ads on popular local and national websites like WSJ.com,

CNN.com, Foxnews.com, ESPN.com, or weather.com, or your ads could show on your local newspaper, TV, or radio stations' websites. The more targeted your ad is to your prospect, the better they work. The downside is that your prospects are not looking for you. They are doing their thing online or offline, and your ad is interrupting. Hopefully it catches their attention in an effective way.

The very first intrusive advertisement was by Bulova Watch Company in 1926 on a radio broadcast, announcing, "At the tone, it's eight o'clock, Bulova Watch Time," an announcement heard by millions of Americans. It must have worked really well because Bulova continued to pioneer the use of radio advertising well into the 1940s. Bulova Watch Company sponsored all the top 20 radio shows of the time and dramatically grew their business. Then, on July 1, 1941, Bulova was presented with the opportunity to have the very first advertisement on broadcast television. It aired before a baseball game between the Brooklyn Dodgers and the Philadelphia Phillies on the New York television station WNBT. The advertisement cost Bulova anywhere from $4 to $9 (reports vary). The ad simply displayed a WNBT test pattern modified to look like a clock with the hands showing the time. The Bulova logo, with the phrase "Bulova Watch Time," was shown in the lower right-hand quadrant of the test pattern while the second hand swept around the dial for one minute. This was the beginning of trillions of dollars spent on visual intrusive advertisements.

Intrusive ads are excellent for branding. Many iconic niches like auto, colas, and fast food primarily use intrusive marketing.

However, intrusive marketing is also great for introducing new concepts to people, maybe something they didn't know they needed. Innovative technology is often introduced by intrusive marketing. Things like smartphones, solar panels, and robotic vacuums have capitalized on the power of intrusive media.

In my award shop, I can push ads specifically targeted to "brides to be" about things they didn't think about, like personalized wedding favors. Or I can target dog owners for new pet tags or wine drinkers with a personalized wine bottle opener. My prospects weren't looking for these things, but my ad was targeted directly at them, and it intrigued them enough to click through for more information. Obviously, these leads are nowhere near as hot as someone searching for you, but they do convert. It is another fantastic way to get people to know your business.

Geofencing

Geofencing is a form of hyper intrusive marketing where you draw a virtual fence around a building or small geographical area that you want to target with online ads. This is not to be confused with simple "geo-targeted" ads where you target a mile radius or larger. Geofencing ads are much more focused and will only show to those people who are within that "fence" line. This can be an immensely powerful way of intrusively pushing ads in front of targeted prospects. For instance, lawyers can geofence hospitals. It's a modern form of ambulance chasing, but as of now, in most states, the bar association has approved it.

The key to making geofenced ads work is to design ads that are extremely relevant to your audience. You must get their attention. For instance, I can run geofenced ads around the local Association of Realtors building that says, "Hey Realtor, if you do not have a nametag, shame on you. You are a professional; get your Realtor nametags here." Yes, it is kind of creepy when this kind of hyper targeting happens to you, but it works nonetheless.

Time-Lapse Marketing

Along the same lines as geofencing, you can buy historical pixel data for specific locations. For instance, if you own a restaurant, you can actually run ads to anyone who has been inside of one of your competitors' locations sometime in the past week, month, or year.

With all these options of marketing and hundreds more, if you scrape away all the minutia, there are really only two numbers you need to know if your marketing is successful. 1.) Average lifetime value of your customer (LTV). 2.) Cost per acquisition (CPA): how much does it cost you to acquire a customer? Once you have an accurate read on these two things, nothing stops you from dramatically scaling your business (assuming that your CPA is lower than the gross profit of your LTV).

CHAPTER 8

LIKE

I turned out liking you more than I originally planned.
− Anon

30K FOOT VIEW

In our customer journey of Know, Like, Trust, Try, Buy, and Evangelize, the next step after someone gets to know you and your company is to get them to like you. From the beginning of commerce to about 75 years ago, this step was not necessary. Rarely could you find more than one merchant selling what you needed. You didn't have a choice.

There was only one merchant who sold flour, one who sold gas or kerosene, one who sold clothes, one who sold bread, and so on. You had to buy from that person even if you hated them. It was impossible to buy around them. It really has only been about the last 60–70 years where we truly have open options at our fingertips. If you don't like a merchant, you don't have to use them. Every single niche in every market is now genuinely saturated. If you can think of one that isn't saturated, let me know. I am looking to dominate another market.

According to the American Bar Association's Profile of the Legal Profession, in 1991 there were 805,872 lawyers. In 2022, that number has grown to 1,327,010, a staggering 39 percent growth in a niche that was supposedly highly saturated 30 years ago. The interesting part is each lawyer must be licensed in the state(s) they practice. Well, there are now many firms stepping over multiple state lines to practice. Several "mega" firms are now practicing in dozens of states, some claiming all fifty states. If you opened your law firm in Pensacola, Florida, 30 years ago, you may have had a few other general lawyers, and certainly no subniche lawyers. But today, competition has gone through the roof with local, state, and national firms vying for the same cases you automatically got 30 years ago.

If you have ever driven through the south, especially Alabama, you have undoubtably seen the billboards of the big personality personal injury lawyer Alexander Shunnarah. At one point in the past couple of years, he had over 2,500 billboards and a marketing budget of $18 million a year. At his peak, his office was fielding 1,500 phone calls a day. Those are leads that used to go to the local attorneys.

Out-of-state attorneys used to refer a case to local firms but are now opting to keep them and work them. The term "starving attorney" didn't exist ten years ago. Now you see them on the side of the road with cardboard signs. Fierce competition isn't unique just to the legal niche; it is unquestionably fierce for all small businesses.

Other niches are not immune to multistate competition. Many HVAC and plumbing companies now advertise across state lines. They book the appointment and subcontract the work to someone local and take a nice cut of the pie. There are at least a half dozen online "leads" companies in the home services niche that do nothing but advertise online and sell leads to local businesses. This drives up local marketing costs for true local businesses.

A quick Google search for what you do in your market will reveal the staggering truth that you have competition, lots of it. As an example, I searched "personal injury lawyer in Pensacola." There were 57 lawyers in the Local Services Ads, 129 lawyers in the maps, and 659,000 other relevant pages in the search results. Another example: I searched "dentist Chico, Ca," and maps came up with 155 listings. A search for "accounting firms

Nashville, TN" brings up 119 maps listings. There is no doubt your local business has fierce competition as well. The question is, How do you get them to pick you? It's no longer enough for them to just know you; they must also like you in order to pick you.

The psychology behind why people choose one company or product over another is extremely complex, with many moving parts. I will endeavor to simplify the reasoning by breaking down how different types of people are motivated and demotivated; then we will match that with the six reasons someone would choose a business.

First, we need to understand the diverse types of people.

Around the year 460 BC, Hippocrates suggested that humans had a "persona," which comprised four distinct temperaments. He suggested that whichever fluid was more dominant in a person determined their "humor," and thus their different personality.

In 1879, Wilhelm Wundt, who is known as the father of psychology, became the first person to draw a clear-cut distinction between the human body and a human personality theory.

The late 1800s began the rise of the psychodynamic approach and drastically changed the way that we viewed and understood personality in social situations with a group of people.

By the early 1900s, Sigmund Freud suggested that our personality was a lot more complex than originally suggested and that our behavior—and personality—is driven by our innate drives and needs. Freud founded the psychodynamic approach, which is the theory that human functioning is based upon the interaction of drives and forces within the person, particularly in their unconscious, and between the different structures of the personality.

Later, Carl Jung proposed that there are only four human personality preferences: sensing, intuition, thinking, and feeling, and that these influence our personality. The mid-1900s led to an increased interest in personality testing and assessments, especially in the workplace.

The first modern personality test was the Woolworth personal data sheet; it was used by the U.S. Army to detect which recruits would be susceptible to shell shock.

Since the mid-1900s, personality tests and assessments have skyrocketed. People are now remarkably familiar with personality quizzes such as the Myers-Briggs test, DiSC, 16 personalities, Big Five, True Colors, and other various IQ and personality tests.

Suffice it to say, biped homo sapiens are utterly unique and complicated, and it's hard to pigeonhole them into groups. However, most of these tests agree that in general, there are four main personality types with dozens of subsets.

Four Personality Types

For the sake of simplicity, I'll use the four birds analogy of DiSC personality types to teach you how to adjust your marketing to attract the different personality types and exactly how to get them to like you and your business.

1.) Eagle (Dominant)

The Eagle personality type is a person who sees from a 30,000 foot view. They are big-picture and visionary. Eagles are also strong willed and decisive, which means they make decisions fast. Eagles are confident and can be dominating, demanding, overbearing, outspoken, sometimes blunt, and direct. Some call them "type A," or "alpha males," or "alpha females." Eagles do not like to get bogged down in the details and want you to get straight to the point. Eagles place emphasis on accomplishing results and getting things done.

Marketing to an Eagle

Your website should have a big and bold call to action above the scroll. Phone calls and form fills work great for an Eagle. On the form fill, don't make them fill out a bunch of details. Name, email, and maybe the phone number is plenty, or you will lose them. Your website should load fast and should be formatted and responsive to mobile because Eagles will not wait around. Your marketing must also quickly answer how you will solve their pain or give them the pleasure they want. You need to connect the dots for them. Nothing esoteric or some obscure branding ad. Tell them what they want to hear, which could be how their problem "is not their fault" or how you can fix their problem fast. They want to see a timeline on how quickly they will see results, and they want to feel confident you will not waste their time.

Once you have an Eagle as a customer or client, you must continue stroking their egos. The relationship cannot get stale. You must push novel items or techniques or shiny things. If you don't give it to them, they will move to someone who will.

Eagles love the spotlight, so you should have them do a video testimonial about your company on how you solved their problem. Essentially you killed two birds with one stone, (see what I did there). You get a testimonial, and they get to be in the spotlight.

If you do all of this, they will feel comfortable with you, like you, and do business with you.

2.) Parrot (Influencer)

Parrots are colorful and talkative. They want to be heard and seen; they thrive on recognition. They are enthusiastic, charismatic, energetic, influential, persuasive, inspirational, and optimistic and have a positive attitude. Parrots prefer the fast chase and spontaneity. Parrots love good surprises (of course, no one likes unpleasant surprises) that leave lasting impressions. Parrots are open and trusting.

Marketing to a Parrot

Phone numbers and chat windows are critical for parrots because they want to talk with a live person. Make sure someone answers the phone, especially if your marketing is pushing them to call. Patience is not a Parrot's virtue. Respond quickly or they will move on to other shiny things.

When you do talk with a Parrot, enthusiastically answer their questions. They probably already know the answer; they just want human confirmation. When you see them or go to their house or business, make sure you give a genuine compliment. They want you to notice. Always ask about their obnoxious shirt or shoes, their unusual painting, or some obscure photograph or item on their desk—it's there; look for it. They want to tell you the story. Let them. Ask open-ended questions and be prepared for a long-winded answer. But genuinely listen to the answer; they will tell you exactly what they want and how to be sold.

Once you have a Parrot as a customer or client, make sure you ask for feedback and take their advice if you can. Surprise gifts go a long way, but so does a phone call. Just like the Eagle, the Parrot loves the spotlight, so have them do a video testimonial.

3.) Dove (Steadiness)

Lovey, dovey as they say. Doves are about relationships and family values. Doves are loyal, sincere, sympathetic, emotional, compassionate, dependable, cooperative, and supportive. They tend to have calm, deliberate dispositions and don't like to be rushed. Doves are the peacekeepers and hate conflict. They are skittish by nature, but once they trust you, they will completely open up.

Marketing to a Dove

Doves want to know who you are as a person and your contributions to society. Second to your home page, the next page a Dove looks at is the "about us" page. They want to see photos of you, your family, your employees and their background, how long you have owned the business, where you went to school, the organizations you belong to, what awards you have won, what philanthropic endeavors you participate in, even the outside hobbies you enjoy. Doves are looking for common ground, so list every cool thing you are involved with and every cool thing you have done. The third thing Doves will look at are reviews, testimonials, and case studies. They will look at your Google and Yelp reviews and your Better Business Bureau rating. They want to know what others are saying about you, but more than that, they want to see if someone they know has done business with you. If you have photos of you and celebrities, make sure you post them. It could just be local celebrities like the mayor or sheriff or the owner of a local car dealership. If they like those people, they will like you by association. Once you have a Dove as a customer, they will stay loyal to you as long as the status quo does not change. Make sure you call them by name and bring up a previous conversation you had with them. Don't forget to ask about the kids or the dog. Doves will give a written testimonial if asked, and it will be genuine and heartfelt.

4.) Owl (Compliance)

While the feathered owls ask, "Who?" the human Owls ask, "Why?" "How?" and "What if?" Owls are naturally inquisitive and have the ability to consider all possible angles of a situation. Owls are extremely analytical; thus, it takes some time for them to make a decision, and they often fear being wrong. Owls place emphasis on quality and accuracy, expertise, and competency. Owls enjoy their independence and do not like to be out in the open, or front and center. They usually work behind the scenes. Details matter. Get them right.

Marketing to an Owl

Owls have lots of questions. Unfortunately, they hate asking them, which is why you need to preemptively answer everything on your website. Owls want data, statistics, proof, and so on. Owls are naturally distrusting, cautious, and hate risk; that's why they want to read warrantees, guarantees, and they will probably even read the terms of service. The good news is you can bury these things on your website in subpages and they will go out of their way to find them, and it will not annoy the other three types of people. Owls are turned off by sloppiness, disorganization, incongruency, and things that are out of date. If you have misspelled words on your website, Owls are gone. If you have images that don't load or are not formatted correctly on mobile, Owls are gone. They will look at your copyright on the bottom of your website, and it better be current. If you have coupons or events, they need to be current. Owls also want to see your licenses, certifications, and other training, they want to see the associations you belong to, and past accomplishments and achievements. Owls will definitely do their research and probably will look at three to five competitors before deciding. Owls will argue they only make decisions based off logic. This is mostly true, at least more than any other personality type. However, emotions are always involved in decisions. They will choose you if you give them the answers they are looking for on your website and in your marketing.

Once you have an owl as a customer or client, you must continue giving them data. Owls want organization, structure, and they want the details. Send them reports, stats, invoices; they want to see all of it. Owls are extremely loyal, as long as you don't break their trust; keep delivering with consistency and no surprises, and they will stay with you. Never fail to deliver on what you have promised.

It's hard to get an owl to give you a testimonial, but if you can show analytically the improvements you have made for them, they may sign off on it and you can use that data for a case study on your website.

Obviously, we would be naive to believe people actually fit perfectly into one of these four bird types, most of us are a combination. But this analogy works nicely for the purpose of adjusting our marketing to get people to like us.

Now that we know and understand the four types of people, we can strategically and purposefully change our marketing to speak directly to them. As the indelible Dan Kennedy says, "Speak to the dog in the language of the dog" or in our case, speak to the bird in their bird language. Your marketing should always have the four personality types in mind. The good news is many of the persuasive tactics we will talk about in this book cross over to all personality types.

IN THE TRENCHES
Six Reasons Someone Would "Like" and
Choose One Business over Others

There have been dozens of studies on why a customer would choose one business over another. When you boil it all down, a person's decision to use your business over another business stems from only these six things.

1. **Commonality:** Given the choice, the decision to use a business could be based off commonality. This could simply mean their friend or relative works there, or they recommend the business because they have used them before. Referrals are a powerful reason a prospect would choose a business. Other forms of commonalities could come from any number of common values, beliefs, location, history, and so on. Classic sales training and persuasion classes correctly teach that you must find common ground to lower the prospects' defenses. Common ground is usually the most powerful deciding factor on whether or not they like you. I know this seems overly shallow, but it's verifiably true. You should strategically and purposefully post common ground items on your Google listing, your website, and social media. Unfortunately, most local business websites have a generic half a paragraph on the "about us" page and nothing personally about them on social media or their Google listing. Please help your prospects find the information they want; I promise you it will pay dividends. Let me give you some specific things you should do to form a commonality bond with your website visitors.

I briefly mentioned your "about us" page earlier in the Dove personality type. As you are well aware by now, people do business with people they know, like, and trust. When prospects click through to your website, they are trying to research you a little more and find out who you are and what you stand for. Because of time constraints, prospects who come to your webpage really have only one motive at first: to sort you into one of two categories. They like you or they don't. Knowing this, you should make every effort to help the visitor find common ground as fast as possible, because it's a powerful way to get them to like you.

Your "about us" page should have your complete bio with photos of you, your family, your pets, your hobbies, and so on.

You should also have a bio for every employee. I know this could be cumbersome, especially because some businesses have a revolving door. But this will serve two purposes. One, your employees will appreciate the recognition, and it shows you are glad to have them on the team. Two, each employee will post their school, associations, and hobbies. This opens up many more opportunities for prospects to find common ground.

Other important things to put on your bio are the associations you are involved with. When I teach from the stage or on zoom, I will usually bring up that I'm the past president of my Rotary club. Undoubtedly there will be other Rotarians in the audience, and we automatically have a bond. If you donate time and money to the humane society and a prospect who cares about cats and dogs sees that on your bio, they will automatically like you more. Make sure you list all your philanthropic endeavors on your bio.

You should also post your alma mater, your fraternity or sorority, or any other club you may have been a part of.

Other things you should have on your "about us" page and another terrific way of finding common ground is your military background. Please post your rank and years of service, as this is an extremely powerful bond. Studies also show that the majority of non-military prospects will respect you more for your service. This is absolutely true for me; your stock automatically goes up in my eyes if you served in the military.

Another must-have on your website is accolades. In my experience, most business owners suck at bragging about themselves; however, your awards and accomplishments are a fantastic way to get prospects to like you more. Psychological studies tell us that people are naturally drawn to successful people. The same is true for successful businesses. Show photos of your awards and certifications, big and small. Show them all.

Okay, now that a prospect has found some sort of common ground, we must overcome the next few hurdles as well.

2. **Reputation/Trust:** This is a huge determining factor why some people will choose a business. We will discuss how to build trust extensively in the next chapter.

3. **Price/Value:** Price is definitely a determining factor but less so than most business owners realize. Recent studies show only 9 to 14 percent of consumers will choose a business primarily because of price. Everyone takes price into consideration, but it's usually third or fourth on the list of importance. If people switch to you because of price, they will switch to someone else because of price. In the end, you need to justify your price with the quality and the value you deliver.

One of our auto repair clients has a sign on the wall that says, "Done Right, Fast, Cheap—You Can Only Pick Two." Most people nod in understanding when they figure it out. If you want it done right and fast, it won't be cheap. If you want it fast and cheap, it won't be done right. If you want it done right and cheap, it won't be fast. I have always had a hard time with that concept. Why can't it be all three? I wholeheartedly believe that if you do the job better than expected and faster than expected, the price will seem like a bargain because of the value you bring.

4. **Convenience:** Convenience could be the location of the business. This matters more to quick, recurring purchases, like restaurants, gas stations, hair and nail salons, car washes, and so on. Proximity has little bearing for businesses that come to you like plumbers, roofers, lawn care, and so forth. Also, most people would have no

problem driving across town to see their accountant, lawyer, or dentist once or twice a year.

Convenience also means the complexity of the transaction, the amount of friction when doing business with you, the speed of delivery of your product or service, and so on. This will absolutely factor in their decision on which business to use. When we bought our award shop, the former owner had the store hours open 8 a.m. to 6 p.m. Tuesday to Friday. Most of the other award shops in town had similar hours. We opened Mondays and took away that friction. Our sales immediately went up by over 15 percent. You may know the story behind One Hour Heating and Air's guarantee. Almost everyone has experienced the frustrations of having to wait at home all day for a service company to show up. One Hour Heating and Air set themselves apart from the competition by removing that friction with their on-time guarantee: *Always On Time...Or You Don't Pay A Dime!* ®. Do you have friction or bottlenecks in your business? Are there hoops you make your prospects and customers jump through just to do business with you? Be the contrarian in your industry and remove the inconvenient issues. Make it convenient for your customers, and it will catapult your business.

A side note on convenience: unfortunately in Western culture, we are getting lazier, and convenience will often trump price and quality most of the time. Just drive by McDonald's and Starbucks and notice the line around the building.

5. **Uniqueness:** Sometimes you can carve out a unique proposition. Rarely will your product or service be unique, but the way you produce it, package it, or price it can be unique, or the systems you use could produce a unique experience where people would choose your company over others. Marble Slab Creamery and Dippin' Dots are just ice cream shops with a twist. Sport Clips is just a barber shop, but they have a unique way of delivering their product and service. Maybe you can find a unique way to deliver what you do.

6. **Quality:** As rivalry continues to grow, quality will definitely become more important for all industries. Some items are easily distinguishable by the quality of parts. There is certainly a quality difference between a Kia and a Rolls Royce. And there is definitely a quality difference between Charmin Ultra, hypoallergenic 2-ply with aloe and vitamin E toilet paper versus the single-ply Dollar Tree toilet paper (which doubles as 400 grit sandpaper). But most of the time, it's hard to distinguish medium quality from exceptional quality. Usually quality is amplified by packaging, delivery, or presentation.

For service industries, quality can come from the state-of-the-art equipment you use. For instance, plumbers could have the latest acoustic listening equipment for leak detection and waterproof plumbing video camera systems that quickly and easily identify problems that need to be addressed. For chiropractors, you could have the cutting-edge robotized multi-target class four-laser technology, which immediately produces relief of muscle and joint pain. For a sign shop, you could have the latest latex or UV printers in which the colors won't fade and last years longer than solvent printers.

For restaurants, quality could come from technology like order kiosks at the table or an app for table reservations. Other items that will promote quality are amazingly clean bathrooms, nicer serving dishes, and better lighting. These things have nothing to do with the food but dramatically increase the perceived quality.

Quality can also come in the form of presentation. There has been massive debate on the quality of Starbucks coffee. But the presentation and atmosphere certainly allow them to charge three to five times more than a McDonald's coffee.

Presentation can certainly change the perception of quality. We will discuss this a little further in Chapter 16: Order Average.

These six reasons are why prospects will choose your business over another business. All these reasons are things you can strategically and purposefully work on to get more people to "like" your business.

Four Marketing Ways to Get Prospects, Customers, or Clients to Like You

1.) Database Marketing

It is astonishingly sad to me how many businesses don't collect emails or cell phone numbers. Email marketing and short message service (SMS) text marketing are extremely powerful ways to get prospects to take interest in your business and "like" you. I am putting database marketing under the "like" category because usually you acquire their name, email, and cell phone number from the first time they buy from you or inquire about your product or service. You can buy these databases and do cold outreach, but I'm not a fan of it, and the efficacy is nearly zero with current spam filters.

Your business should have a strategic marketing procedure for collecting emails and cell phone numbers. The absolute best way to get a database is from your current customers. They will gladly give it to you if they have had a wonderful experience and plan to come back. Do not be afraid to ask for it. You can also get emails and sometimes cell phone numbers from business cards. If you have acquired cards from networking groups or chamber meetings, you legally have the right to send them an email or text if it was on the card. However, you must have an opt-out selection on both email and text to be compliant.

Once you have a database, start sending useful content. Remember, "database marketing" is under the "like" heading. You need to send them things that will get them to like you more. It could be coupons or BOGOs or free offers, but it could also just be excellent content that actually helps them, and they would actually want to consume. Think about the emails you enjoy reading.

2.) Newsletters

These can be email newsletters, but printed and mailed newsletters are much more powerful. Just like your emails, newsletters should provide valuable content that can actually help your customer or prospect. (By the

way, you should sign up for my newsletter at https://prosperousim.com/
prosperouspartner.) I have seen excellent newsletters from virtually all local
business niches. It would be worth your time if you wrote it yourself, but
there is probably a "done for you" service that you can subscribe to that
will write an excellent newsletter for you.

3.) Public Relations

Most local small businesses will not be able to afford a true public relations
company. However, you can still do some basic public relations on your
own. I am a huge fan of press releases. My agency sends out between 75
and 100 a month for our clients. I have seen the power of them firsthand.

One of our plumbing clients had a technician save a kitten out of a
drainpipe. We sent out a press release to the local media and the Associated Press. It must have been a slow news day because the press release
got picked up by several hundred media and news outlets. They had the
local newspaper and TV station come to interview them. This does not
happen very often, but when it does, the business gets a huge boost in
their business, plus a great boost on their online rankings because the local
media is linking to their website. Obviously, the more newsworthy it is, the
better chance it will have of getting picked up. There are dozens of press
release distribution companies out there. The two best are prweb.com and
newswire.com. But you should absolutely be collecting contact information
for your local media so you can send it locally.

4.) Philanthropic Endeavors

Philanthropy means love of humanity, generosity in all its forms, and is
often defined as giving gifts of "time, talent, and treasure" to help make
life better for other people.

Many large corporations implement Corporate Social Responsibility
(CSR). CSR refers to practices and policies undertaken by corporations that
are intended to have a positive influence on the world and their communi-
ties. The key idea behind CSR is for corporations to pursue other pro-social

objectives, in addition to maximizing profits. Examples of common CSR objectives include minimizing environmental impact, promoting volunteerism among company employees, and donating to charity. Small local businesses can and should implement something similar.

My award shop donates over thirty thousand dollars a year in products and cash to local charities and worthy causes in our area. One of my favorite things we did was in the first year of the COVID pandemic, my award shop partnered with a local radio station and gave away "Act of Kindness" medallions. People from the community would send in nominations of people doing acts of kindness in our community. I was truly blown away by the selfless acts people were doing. I have had dozens of people thank me for recognizing our local heroes.

One of our law firm clients feeds the homeless once a year by cooking hamburgers and hot dogs outside their office. They actually cook it themselves and wait on hundreds of vagrants and homeless people (plus a few media people). This act of kindness costs them thousands of dollars, and there is no doubt this is genuine, and it shows. It builds an enormous amount of goodwill in our community.

There is zero argument that all successful local businesses are highly involved in giving back to their local community. I am not sure if they started giving to their local community once they became successful or if they became successful because they gave to their local community. It does not matter; you should give time and money to your local community because it obviously helps your community and it's the right thing to do. However, the ancillary benefit to doing it is because you can write a press release about it and get the local press to cover it. There is nothing wrong with getting recognition for the wonderful things your business does for your community.

CHAPTER 9

TRUST

If people like you they will listen to you, but if
they trust you, they'll do business with you.
– Zig Ziglar

30K FOOT VIEW

Moving along in our customer journey, once prospects know who you are, and they like you, before they will try you, they must trust you. In fact, as we discussed in the previous chapter, "trust" is a huge percentage of why customers like you and will choose to buy from your business.

Customer feedback has been around long before the internet. The oldest known written complaint was written on a clay tablet around 1750 BC. It is currently kept in the British Museum. It's a complaint from a copper merchant named Nanni to a copper wholesaler named Ea-nasir. Ea-nasir had agreed to sell copper ingots to Nanni. Nanni sent his servant with the money to complete the transaction. The copper was substandard and not accepted. In response, Nanni inscribed the complaint to Ea-nasir about the copper delivery of the incorrect grade and complained that his servant (who handled the transaction) had been treated rudely. He stated that, at the time of writing, he had not accepted the copper but had paid the money for it. Even more fascinating, during excavation of what was believed to be Ea-nasir's dwelling, archaeologists found other tablets that include a letter from a man named Arbituram who complained he had not received his copper yet, while another tablet that says he was tired of receiving bad copper. Obviously, this wholesaler was a shyster, and unfortunately back then there were few other options. But nowadays your reputation is always front and center and usually the first thing people see about you online, and they always have other options.

The first online reviews made their appearance in 1999. There were three main review websites online: Epinions.com, RateItAll.com, and Deja.com. By 2001, Yellow Pages and Citysearch had added online reviews to their already large directory of businesses. In 2002, Google, understanding the power of reviews, bought the Usenet search technology from Deja, which essentially gave them ownership over all of Usenet's online discussion groups and reviews. This quickly put Google in the online review game.

Yelp was founded in 2004 and quickly got into the review fight. By 2005, Yelp revamped their site to allow users to publicly share their reviews, which was a game changer.

In June of 2007, Google made it possible to leave a review for a business on Google Maps. This launched the reputation war because now a business reputation was front and center along with all their competitors.

It took until 2009 before businesses were allowed to publicly respond to reviews on Yelp. Google followed suit in early 2010.

From 2012 to 2017, Facebook was the leader in online business reviews because of the large volume of users of the platform. Yelp was close behind, and both maintained steady growth in those years. However, in early 2017, Google skyrocketed ahead of the competition. According to ReviewTracker's top directories analysis as of mid-2022, Google accounts for 73% of all online reviews worldwide. Yelp 6%, Facebook is around 3%, TripAdvisor 3%, Trust Pilot 3%, Better Business Bureau 1%, and others 11%.

Obviously, business and product reviews are here to stay. My prediction is, in the future, platforms will make it much harder to post fake reviews. The Better Business Bureau has taken the lead in weeding out fake reviews.

It's labor intensive; however, every single review is vetted and verified by the Better Business Bureau (BBB) staff to make sure it's real. If it is negative, they will contact the business owner to see if they would like to write a rebuttal. Amazon is cracking down on fake reviews by verifying that you purchased the item. Even then, they somehow will kick out legitimate reviews if they know that person is related to the seller. My mom's review of my first book was taken down, and she actually read the book!

Amazon has trained us to look at the reviews, sort the bad ones, and read them. If there are too many of the same complaints, we move on to the next product. Unfortunately, people do the exact same thing when looking at your local business. They will check out the reviews if you have any and mostly look for the bad ones.

Bright Local LTD did a very robust Local Consumer Review Survey in January of 2022. https://www.brightlocal.com/research/local-consumer-review-survey/. Their key findings are staggering and simply prove the importance of online reviews.

One of the more astounding findings is that 81 percent of 18- to 34-year-olds and 89 percent of 35- to 54-year-olds trust an online review as much as a friend or family member. Think about that: eight out of ten people would take the recommendation of a complete stranger who wrote a review online (either good or bad) and trust it as much as a friend or family member.

The survey also revealed that 93 percent of consumers used the internet to find a local business in the last year (up from 90 percent in 2020), with 34 percent looking every day. Eighty-seven percent of consumers read online reviews for local businesses, with 52 percent of 18- to 54-year-olds saying they "always" read reviews. Just to give you a mental image and tie this statistic to the previous chapter, usually it's the Doves and Owls that read reviews, which make up about 50 percent of the population. The average consumer reads 10 reviews before feeling able to trust a business, and the average consumer spends 13 minutes and 45 seconds reading reviews before making a decision. Among consumers who read reviews, 96 percent read businesses' responses to reviews (which is why you should always respond to reviews). An overwhelming 95 percent suspect censorship or faked reviews if there are not any negative ones.

The most important review factors in order are:

1. Star rating
2. Legitimacy
3. Recency
4. Sentiment
5. Quantity

Another key finding in the study was the fact that over half (52 percent) of consumers will not use a business if it has less than a 4-star rating. WOW, think about that statistic. It behooves you to get your ratings up. My minimum threshold for our clients is a 4.2 for most industries. For lawyers, it must be 4.7 or higher. For restaurants, it can be a little lower because the average is much lower and because of the sheer volume of reviews. Speaking of volume, according to the same Bright Local LTD study, the top three ranked local businesses had an average of 47 reviews, while those businesses in the seventh to tenth position on Google had only an average of 38 reviews. This is logical because experts believe that review signals can attribute up to 15 percent of the local Google My Business ranking factors.

When my digital marketing agency takes on any new client, after the initial onboarding, we always start with their online reputation. We must get control of their reputation, which means get log ins to every single website that allows reviews, then we take a snapshot of where they are at. We actively monitor 13 different review sites for each client; however, there are dozens more. You would be surprised how many rogue reviews there are out there that business owners have no idea are there. Once we have control and we are able manage their reputation, then we aggressively begin to grow their online reputation and ultimately market their reputation. All other forms of marketing will at best be mute or at worst backfire if you have a bad online reputation or don't have any reputation.

A friend of mine is a fairly new Edward Jones financial advisor. There are dozens of them in our town who have been around for decades, and they have tons of clients. After doing a little research, I realized that most of them had fewer than two reviews on Google, and he had none. I strongly advised him to get at least ten legitimate five-star reviews. I rarely give out specific tactical advice for free anymore. Not because of the money, but because 95 percent of the time they will not do it if they don't have skin in the game. Well, this guy was different. He actually went out and quickly got over 25 legitimate reviews from his clients, family, and friends. To his surprise, it shot him up to number one for over two dozen keywords in Google Maps, including being number one for the search terms "Edward Jones Financial Advisor" and number one for the generic search term "financial advisor" in our town. He has sent me several thank you cards, thanking me every time a new client calls him because they saw his reviews online and he was at the top. In full transparency, his rankings will not last unless he builds his online authority outside of reviews as well. But he can enjoy the boost for a little while.

In our call tracking company, we have saved dozens of recordings of a prospect who says they called the business just because of their reviews. Sometimes your online reviews could be the deciding factor of why they call you versus some other business; it is certainly one of the top three reasons they choose a business. It is well worth your time to strategically acquire legitimate five-star reviews. In most instances, you do not need hundreds of reviews, start with a goal of 20 and try to get to 50 by the end of the year. Here are four ways to get more five-star reviews.

IN THE TRENCHES
Four Ways to Build a Five-Star Reputation

1.) Low-Hanging Fruit

All businesses have what I call "evangelists," which we will learn about in Chapter 12. These are the people who love your business and will go out of their way to promote you. Simply make a list of your top 20 evangelists and personally ask them to leave you a detailed review with a photo on Google and Facebook. Make it extremely easy for them by giving them the direct link to your review pages. To get your direct link to your GBP listing, simply log in to your Google Business Profile page. Click "home" on the top left. Scroll down until you see "Get More Reviews." Then click on the button that says "Share Review Form." This will give you a direct link for your customers to leave you a review. Email or text the link to your top customers and explain to them that their review is especially important to you and will help your business thrive. I'm positive all of them will say yes! The shocking news is statistically only a handful will actually complete the review and have it stick. The key is to follow up and remind them that this is particularly important to you. It's against the terms of service to bribe someone to leave a review. But there is nothing wrong with taking a customer to lunch to say thanks for leaving a review. It is worth that and more.

2.) Email Signature Review Link

Add your direct review link to the bottom of your email signature. Create a template of your company signatures that will include the link to Google reviews with a simple call to action. For example, you can design a signature with a button or simple link text such as: "Review us on Google" or "Share your feedback on Google." One of my email signatures says, "If you were ecstatic with your experience, please let everyone know and leave us feedback here (link to my GBP). If you were anything less than ecstatic, please call me personally."

3.) Post-Purchase Campaign

Create a post-purchase email and text sequence that will automatically trigger an email and text message to each customer after they have done business with you. We use proprietary software that helps follow up with customers through text and email to ask them for their feedback, but this is something you can do manually. In the software, we have what we call a "checkout form" for all our clients. It works especially well for our law firm clients and home services clients. It is an app that triggers a text and email that asks for feedback. Lawyers send this to their clients after their case is handled and they are happiest. For a personal injury lawyer, that is right when you hand them a check from the insurance company or after their bankruptcy hearing or after their divorce is final. For a plumber, it is right when the toilet finally flushes. For a retail store, it is right after they make a purchase. For a dentist, it is when they are still a little loopy from the laughing gas. Your business should also have a consistent, simple strategy to follow up with every happy customer to ask them to leave you a review.

4.) Android Phones Are Your Friend

If you did not know, Android is owned by Alphabet Inc., which is the parent company of Google. There is not an easier way to leave a review on Google than an Android phone, mostly because they are already logged in to Google, so it skips the login process. Most people get stuck trying to log in on an iPhone.

When you are out to dinner with friends or on the golf course or at the round top table at a chamber meeting, tell everyone to take their phones out. Tell them to "Google" your business name, click on your listing in the maps, and scroll down until you see stars. Then tell them to leave you a detailed review. For the ones with an Android phone, there is a huge chance those reviews will stick immediately.

Four Steps to Take After Getting a Bad Review

It's just a matter of time before someone will leave you a negative review. For my agency, part of our reputation marketing package entails a four-step approach when our client gets a negative review. I strongly suggest that you do these four things as well.

1.) Immediately Try to Get Ahold of the Customer

There is a remarkably high percentage chance that the customer will remove the review or change the review if you solve their problem within the first 72 hours. Most customers are reasonable and just want to be heard and know that you are willing to do something to fix the issue. Sometimes all it takes is a phone call from the manager or owner. I strongly recommend you do whatever it takes to make them happy. It is worth thousands, maybe tens of thousands of dollars to not have a one-star review.

A few years ago, I had a plumbing client, and the owner was extremely pompous and egocentric. He was personally very rude and mean to a customer (well, many customers). I tried to help with damage control, but he refused to apologize or try to make amends. Unfortunately for him, this lady was well versed in online review platforms. She destroyed his reputation in about a week.

From what I could find, she left reviews on over seven reviews sites with two paragraphs of detail. The reviews started a snowball effect and dozens of other customers came forward and left reviews on how rude he was. It took a few months, but I am positive it was the crux that in the end cost him his business. In fact, he ultimately had to change the name of his business and start all over with a new brand.

Before he sabotaged his business, he was spending over twenty thousand a month on Google Ads, and we were starting to dominate in the local rankings. He was getting a ton of booked appointments, and we were doubling his business every six months. He could not hire enough technicians and buy enough vans to keep up. His business would have brought in well over ten million a year if he had swallowed his pride.

2.) Flag the Review

If we cannot get ahold of the customer or if they are unwilling to change the review, the second line of defense is to try to get the review removed. We flag the review (a bunch of times), which will usually trigger a manual human examination of the review. This mostly only works for Google and Yelp. In their terms of service, they will pretty much remove a review if there is anything that is perceived shady, threatening, or immoral. You can sometimes get reviews removed that have bad misspellings or slang. But they will almost definitely remove them if there are cuss words, threats or insults or racists remarks. We have not tracked it as much as we should, but my guess is we get around 25 to 30 percent of the negative reviews removed, maybe more. It is definitely worth the time it takes to try.

3.) Respond to the Review

At this point, our response really is not for the person that left it. It is for all the prospects that will read the negative review in the future. According to that same Bright Local LTD survey, 22 percent of consumers will "not likely at all" use a business that has not responded to reviews. An additional 35 percent will "not very likely" use the business with no review responses. The conclusion is that 57 percent of your prospects will probably not use your business if you do not respond to reviews. I think that's plenty of incentive to leave a response, but it must be the right response.

The absolute worst thing you can do is try and argue the situation online, even if you are right. I have personally been involved in an online argument with a customer over a review a lady left that was an outright lie. I made the mistake of trying to correct her and it escalated, and she fabricated even more lies. The problem is now when people read the responses, they have to take one side or the other, and I am sure some people actually believe her (even though she's verifiably bat guano crazy).

If I could do it over, I would remove my emotions, stop the damage online, and try to at least neutralize the review. Online review platforms are the absolute wrong place to argue with someone; it is definitely a losing situation for the business owner. Sometimes you can negate a negative review by taking the high road and explaining nicely how you tried to rectify the situation. For instance, you may respond by saying:

"I am terribly sorry to read about your unpleasant experience. We strive hard to have excellent customer service as you can see from all our other reviews, but it looks like we fell short with you. We have refunded your money and come back out and fixed the problem for free. I have documented your complaint to make sure this doesn't happen again. If there is something else we can do to rectify the situation, please call me personally 555-555-5555, Owner of AAA Locksmith."

A year from now, when someone reads the review and your response, they will at least feel that you tried and are willing to go out of your way to make them happy.

4.) Dilute the Bad Review

By diluting, we mean moving it down the page by getting new five-star reviews. You must be careful to follow Google's terms of service. You can ask individual customers to submit reviews, but Google review guidelines forbid "soliciting reviews from customers in bulk." That's okay. It is worth asking each customer individually to leave you a five-star review.

That is our four-step damage control if one of our clients gets a negative review, and it works remarkably well. It will do the same for you.

After you have control of your online reviews, you should focus on making your website more trustworthy, because after reviews, a substantial percentage of prospects will check out your website next. Here are a few trust factors you can easily add to your website.

Four Must-Have Website Trust Factors

1.) Credibility

Unless your URL is amazon.com, most people will rightfully be skeptical of your website. Here are three ways to gain online credibility.

Esthetics: Your website must look professional and not like a fifth-grade computer class project. You have about three to five seconds for prospects to form an opinion about your business. Your website must look professional with a structured, responsive layout, matching color and font themes, easy navigation menus, plus professionally edited photos. Your photos should not be some stock photo you buy online but real-life photos of you, your business, your staff, your fleet, and anything else that will prove you are a legit local business. These photos need to be unique, not blurry or grainy, but professionally taken and professionally edited. It makes a difference.

Also, I know this seems petty, but I must mention two annoying things that I find on the majority of websites I research. This first thing is misspellings. I have software that crawls the entire website and finds potential misspellings. I would guess that over eight out of ten times, I find at least one misspelling, which is embarrassing and lowers your credibility. The second thing could be perceived as petty but is especially important. Nothing says stagnation more prominently to Google and prospects than an out-of-date copyright. Make sure your copyright at the bottom of the page is the current year. It's baffling to me how many websites that have a copyright are three, four, or five years out of date.

Google has acknowledged that an out-of-date copyright is a negative signal in their ranking algorithm, with the theory being that you must not have updated the site in a while. (I wonder how many of you quickly just looked at your website to see what the date of your copyright is.)

Backend Coding/Hosting: Your website should be up to date, with little to no errors. If it's built in Word-Press, make sure you are running the latest version with up-to-date plugins. If it is built in HTML, make sure your developers have your website up to date with the standards of the World Wide Web Consortium (W3C). Hosting is another behind-the-scenes issue that the majority of small businesses have. It's critical that your website loads fast on mobile and desktop. (Use the Google PageSpeed Insights tool from Chapter 4, "Toolset.") You probably won't get a perfect score, but you should be above 75 for both mobile and desktop. The report will tell you exactly what you need to do to fix it.

Most SMB's websites are held on what is called "shared" hosting, which means you share the same IP address as other sites you share hosting with. IP stands for Internet Protocol address and is essentially the computer address of a hosting server, or in this case, where your website resides. It's expressed as a series of four numbers (each between 0 and 255) separated by dots. For example, **64.62.209.175.** Starting on the far left is the A block, then B block, then C block, then D block.

Most web development companies do not talk about how many other websites share your hosting. Shared hosting is inexpensive, but that is the only benefit. The problem with shared hosting depends on how many other sites are sharing it—your website will slow down, and you may be sharing a spot in a bad neighborhood. Google most definitely frowns upon P.P.C websites, (Porn, Pills, Casino). You very well could be sharing the same address as a porn site.

One of our customers—a carpet cleaning company—had a website that shared the same IP address with over one hundred other websites. In fact, every website that developer made was hosted on the same shared hosting. They shared their IP with all their local competitors that the developer also designed, including dozens of other local businesses and a few shady neighbors.

Once we took them on as a client and moved them over to our hosting, like clockwork, their PageSpeed more than doubled, and in just over a week, their rankings went up dramatically. My agency only allows five websites per "D" block IP address. Our large clients that have lots of pages, large videos, and lots of traffic get their own dedicated server with only their website hosted on that IP address. Of course, a dedicated server costs a little more, but it's worth it.

Trust Icons/Seals: Your website should have multiple trust icons on the home page or footer. This could be your business license, your certifications, your chamber membership, or your membership of your niche's association. Third-party accreditations are excellent trust factors. You should also have trust seals prominent on your footer. These are logos of prominent independent and trustworthy authorities that enable you to borrow their credibility as your own. For instance, a study by Digital Marketer shows that satisfaction guarantees and trust seals, even the inexpensive ones, boost conversions by up to 28 percent. Some examples of trust seals you could use are Web of Trust, GoDaddy Site Seal, Norton Secured, McAfee Secure, Hacker Safe, PayPal Verified, Veri-Sign, TRUSTe Certified Privacy, VerifiedSeller.org, SafesiteCertified.org, PrivacyVerified.org, 100% Satisfaction Guarantee, Visa/Mastercard/Amex. Most industries have verified seals of trust. Law firms should use Avvo ratings seal, National Board of Advocacy seal, and their state bar association seal. Accountants should have their American Institute of CPAs seal; Chiropractors should use their accreditation seals, and so on. My absolute favorite trust seal is the BBB logo. It can increase conversions by up to 17 percent. Obviously, you cannot use it unless you are accredited. If you are not, get accredited. Just the increased conversions make it worth the cost. Put the seal prominently at the footer of your website linking back to your accreditation and watch your conversions go up.

2.) Approachability

The next critical thing you must have on your website to gain people's trust is your phone number. Your number should be prominent on every page, in addition to other contact information including your business address, business hours, and other ways to contact you. I strongly recommend you use a local phone number and not a toll-free number.

There really is no reason for toll-free numbers anymore. Millennials do not even know what they are. In fact, recent studies from Google Ads show that a local number will convert over 30 percent better than a toll-free number for service SMBs. The reasoning is most service industries have competing lead capture companies who are aggressively marketing in their city, and they try to pretend they are local, but they usually have a toll-free number.

When you call the number, it puts you in some sort of recorded runaround that asks for all your details. It then sells your lead info to three or more local businesses, all of which will promptly call and vie for your business. Some people don't mind this, but the majority hate it and just simply want to talk to a local business.

Live chat and chatbots help prospects feel comfortable so that they can approach you with questions. It is akin to walking into a box store and someone asking you if they can help you. Most of the time, you do not need their help, but when you do, you are glad they are there.

We also have call tracking phone numbers on most of our clients, which allows for texting. Prospects text questions all the time. Make it as easy as possible for prospects to get ahold of you. You must be approachable.

3.) Frequently Asked Questions (FAQs)

Customers have questions and objections. A robust "frequently asked questions" (FAQ) page is a helpful way to give customers straight answers to their questions. Over 50 percent of your prospects (the Doves and Owls) do not particularly want to call you to ask questions, but they do have questions. I strongly recommend you have a full FAQ page with the ten questions that your prospects and customers always ask, plus another ten questions your prospects and customers should ask but don't. This is different for each industry, but it is important to handle the hardest question you get. Some of the questions are actually rejections, and you need to have the appropriate rebuttal.

Make sure you have thorough and honest answers for all questions even if it might look negative to your business. For instance, a local auto repair shop charges 25 to 50 percent more for repairs than the repair shop down the road. The business owner handles this objection directly on his website by acknowledging that they are certainly more expensive per hour; however, they have state-of-the-art equipment, and their certified master mechanics each have decades of experience. Plus, each mechanic has a highly trained apprentice who assists in every repair.

Combine that with the fact they only use genuine parts or original equipment manufacturer (OEM) parts, never used or aftermarket parts. The culmination of these things allows them to do the job right the first time in about half the time it takes most repair shops. They get you your car back, usually the same day or the next day, even if it's a major repair. You do not have to wait a week or so to get your car back. They even guarantee the parts and labor for three years. This auto repair shop continues to grow and is extremely busy even though they plainly state they will be more expensive.

What about your business? Is there something you need to address that may be construed as a negative? Make sure you handle issues openly and plainly on your website; this will absolutely build trust.

4.) Testimonials/Case Studies
Your website should always have current testimonials and case studies. Sprinkle a few on your home page with a link to a page with as many as

you can get. You should also have a link in your main menu and your footer. Keep in mind that it's one of the first things people will look for on your website, and some people will read every one of them.

Testimonials are usually presented in an interview style, in a quote form, where the customer briefly outlines how your product or service improved their lives. You can use some of your more detailed Google reviews.

A case study is more in-depth than a customer testimonial. A case study should tell the whole story of where they were before working with you or using your product. A case study needs to quantify the customers' pain either in time, money, or lack of happiness, then explain what happened when they started working with you or your product. The case study should show the progression of their success and how you helped them get there. The best case studies have lots of personality, specific stats, and direct quotes from the customer.

The most powerful testimonials and case studies are on video. Video is simply more memorable and much more believable. You don't need a whole lot of video reviews or case studies to benefit from them. Aim for one and build up from there. If you cannot get a video from your customer, at least get a photo of them with you and/or your product. This will give the testimonial more validity.

Now that we have gotten our prospects to know, like, and trust us, the courting stage is over. It is time to get intimate. It is time for them to "try" us.

CHAPTER 10

TRY

30K FOOT VIEW

O nce a prospect gets to know, like, and trust your business, they will then find an opportunity to try your business. What I mean by "try" is they will simply take the next simplest step to dip their toe in to test the waters. It is critical at that moment that they have a wonderful experience. This is their first transaction with your business, and you need to deliberately make sure it will not be their last time using your business.

IN THE TRENCHES
Four Ways to Get Prospects to Try Your Business

1.) Free Trial/Sampling

Try it before you buy it is an excellent way to get a prospect to "try" your business. This gives them a chance to actually try your product or service and to experience it without risk.

SAAS (software as a service) products almost always use a free trial. This is a win-win situation. There is no risk to the consumer, and it usually does not cost the developer anything.

We offer a 14-day free trial on call tracking. During that time, we help customers set up their first phone number and track their first call. We make sure they see all the features we offer and connect the dots on exactly how it will help their business. There is an extremely high probability they will continue with the service after the trial period.

Product sampling is a little riskier for the business owner because there is an expense.

Food sampling has been around for decades, and it still works. Some reports say that a food sample can increase sales by 25 to 30 percent. If you have ever walked through the food court in the mall, there is a high probability of someone handing you some teriyaki chicken on a toothpick. Most partakers do not buy a plate. However, judging by the line, it's still well worth handing out samples.

In the late 1870s, Benjamin Babbitt, an entrepreneur and soap manufacturer, ran the first business documented to capitalize on product sampling. The soap was sold from brightly painted street cars with musicians, which helped lead to the phrase "get on the bandwagon." They would hand out tiny samples of the soap for free and say, "A fair trial is all I ask for it." Babbitt was confident that once someone tried the soap, they would come back and buy from him consistently. It worked perfectly, and he quickly became one of the largest soap manufacturers in the world.

2.) Giveaways

This is not sampling; giveaways are where your business gives away a complete product or service. There are many opportunities to do this, but you must be strategic so that you can get the most value for your business. Most large charities will do a silent auction at their annual banquet. You can give them your product or service to auction off and get your business in front of dozens of highly influential people in your community. The local chamber of commerce also likes to do giveaways every month at their meetings. Just make sure the winners have a wonderful experience.

I had some special business cards made for my award shop. On the back, I have a coupon for a free engraved pen, no purchase necessary; you simply must come to my store. When I go to networking meetings or chamber meetings, I hand them out to people who have never been to my store. My motive is to get people to see my 6,500-square-foot store and get them to realize we do a lot more than sell little plastic trophies. When the people come to redeem the offer, I show them around the store and impress them with all the cool, personalized items we sell that have nothing to do with trophies. Almost all of them buy something immediately or soon after.

3.) Coupons

Anyone who knows me knows that I absolutely despise coupons. It stems from the fact that when I was a broke college student, I had a buy one meal get one meal half off coupon for a nice local restaurant. I carefully calculated the price of the meals, plus drinks and tax and tip. I only had 20 dollars, and I was on a first date. As you probably guessed, the coupon was not valid. For whatever reason, the waiter belittled me in front of my date and of course I did not have enough money to cover the full price. I was completely mortified and to state the obvious, I never got a second date. I vowed I would never use a coupon again, and I certainly never went back to that restaurant.

Since then, I have seen it dozens of times: people trying to use a coupon only to be demeaned and completely disappointed. Unfortunately, these businesses are unknowingly doing irrevocable harm to their reputation.

All that said, coupons absolutely will get new customers to "try" your business, but you must be strategic about using them or they will backfire like my experience did. If you decide to use a coupon, please make sure your employees realize this is part of your marketing, and the entire point of a coupon is to get someone to come "try" your business, usually for the first time. That is their first impression of you.

You should make sure all your customers have an amazing experience, but especially first-time customers. If they do, the likelihood of them coming back goes up dramatically. However, if they have an unpleasant experience, you've probably lost them forever.

Chick-fil-A trains their employees to genuinely say, "Thank you for using a coupon today." This is not happenstance; they know full well that many people have had bad experiences using a coupon.

Just like a guarantee, coupons should have as few conditions as possible. If there are too many hoops to jump through, people will not use them, or if they do, the likelihood of them being confused on the conditions goes way up, which of course leads to a terrible experience.

Obviously the higher the value of the coupon, the higher the redemption rate. Buy one get one works great, as does gift with purchase. Ten percent off, not so much, unless it's for a house or a car.

4.) Joint Venture/Partnerships

A joint venture (JV) partner is a business arrangement in which two or more parties agree to pool their resources for the purpose of accomplishing a specific task. There may be an opportunity for your company to partner with another company to get new customers to try your product or service. Lawyers partner with chiropractors and doctors to help them build a personal injury case. The chiropractors reciprocate by sending leads to the lawyer of patients who may need legal representation.

All successful Realtors have JV partners with mortgage lenders, banks, and credit unions who send them leads of people who are pre-qualified to buy a house. The Realtor will send leads back to them of those people who don't have financing in place. Realtors also partner with appraisers, home inspectors, pest control, landscaping, movers, remodeling companies, and so on.

Many hotels have JV agreements with local restaurants and tourist attractions.

In my award shop, we have JV agreements with a bunch of sign shops, print shops, gift shops, and promotional product salespeople for us to make their signs, nametags, gifts, and so on. We white-label our products to their customers or simply wholesale it to them.

CHAPTER 11

BUY

30K FOOT VIEW

Moving along in our customer journey, once a prospect has "tried" your business, they are now technically a customer. But of course, you do not want that to be the end of the relationship. The term "buy" in this situation means to continue to buy from you—repeat business—and it means buy deep, to move all their budget in your category over to you.

According to a study done by Bain & Company, 60 to 80 percent of customers who describe themselves as satisfied never use that business again. How can that be? Often, it's due to a lack of connection; other times it is simply because you did not ask. SMBs want to do everything they can to get a repeat customer, not just a one-off.

Successful restaurant owners know that it is fairly easy to get you to try their food once. The hard part is to get you to come frequently. Successful financial advisors understand that 95 percent of their new clients will not move all their money over to them at first. They must prove themselves before their client will move over their entire fortune.

IN THE TRENCHES
Three Ways to Get Customers to Buy Repeatedly

1.) Incentivize

Coupons, gift certificates, and free vouchers work to get prospects to try your business; they also work to get them back again.

Jon Taffer from the TV show *Bar Rescue* gives us some humbling stats about repeat customers in the restaurant business. If a customer comes to your establishment and has a flawless experience, the statistical likelihood of them coming back is only 40 percent. Even on the second visit, if that customer comes back and has an equally positive experience, there is now a 42 percent chance that they will return for a third visit. Only slightly higher, but an important setup for the third visit. Then a positive experience on the third visit will result in a now over 70 percent likelihood of them becoming a loyal customer. When Taffer is asked how to increase those percentages, he loves to teach the red napkin technique. You must market to three visits, not one. Taffer says to give out free rib dinner coupons. Then when customers come in, the waiter gives them a red napkin, which signifies to staff that this customer is a first-time visitor to the restaurant. The staff makes sure they have an excellent experience and then the manager or owner of the restaurant asks if they loved their meal, then says, "If you love that, you must try my chicken. Here's $5 off my chicken," and hands them a handwritten coupon on the back of his business card. When they come back the second time and the waiter sees the business card coupon, they know that this is their second time to the restaurant. They once again make sure they have an exceptional experience, then at the end ask if they are full. When they say yes, they say, "Well next time you have to try my cheesecake." Then, give them another coupon for a free piece of cheesecake. Now after the third time of having a wonderful experience, there is over a 70 percent chance they will become loyal customers.

Plumbing, HVAC, and electric companies can incentivize repeat business by giving limited warranties and discounts programs to call them if something goes wrong. After you fix their issue the first time, you can put stickers on the hot water heater or on the air handler or the electric panel that says, "STOP, before you call someone else, call us. This equipment may be under warranty." You could add a little more incentive to call you by giving an additional 10 percent off if you worked on this unit before.

If you own a business that customers will need multiple times per year, like a chiropractor, dentists, hair/nail salon, auto mechanic, pest control, lawn care, pool cleaning, pressure washing, and so on, you need to schedule the next appointment right when you're done with the first one. Put the appointment in your CRM and send them reminders.

This will dramatically increase the likelihood of them coming back.

2.) Create Events

Events could mean a physical event at your location or an offsite event. It could also mean an online event, a seasonal or holiday event, or a promotional event. By event, I mean something a little different than the ordinary.

Watch the marketing calendar of any national brand and you will see they love to have events where their promotional calendars are full. The same should apply to your business. Starbucks always has a nice bump in sales when the "seasonal" pumpkin spice drinks come out. Both Lowe's and Home Depot increased weekend sales with DIY workshops events, and McDonald's loves their scratch-off games like Monopoly because they get customers to come back more often.

There is literally at least one national holiday every single day of the year. Here's the holiday's for the U.S. in 2023 https://calendarr.com/united-states/observances-2023/.

My favorite is December 30, international bacon day, which everyone should celebrate.

3.) Re-Skin the Business (Last-Ditch Effort)

I have seen dozens of businesses on the verge of bankruptcy do a complete turnaround by overhauling their business. It could be something as simple as introducing a new menu, a new chef, or a sign that says under new management or new ownership. If you are in a service industry, you could advertise "all new equipment" or "new satisfaction guarantee." Sometimes you must get more drastic and do a complete rebrand of your business or change your location. Fortunately, when businesses make these changes, past customers who vowed they would never go back usually will give you another shot to see what's changed. Hopefully, you fixed their original concerns. My wife and I went to a highly recommended steak place in our small town when we first moved here about 19 years ago, and we had a horrible experience. Someone gave us free gift certificates, and we still would not go. About a year ago, they put out a banner that said, "Under new ownership," so we gave them another try, and it was surprisingly good. We will probably go there once every couple of months now.

We will discuss how to increase the frequency of sales in more depth in Chapter 17.

CHAPTER 12

EVANGELIZE

30K FOOT VIEW

T he entire goal of the customer journey is to turn a prospect into customer, a repeat customer, an evangelist. An evangelist is an advocate, a promoter, someone who would go out of their way to tell others about you, your business, and your product or service. Fred Reichheld, the loyalty expert, simplified everything when he invented the net promoter score. The net promoter score (NPS) is a survey with only one question. This one question alleviates the need for all other questions.

This ultimate question simply asks, "Would you recommend us to a friend?" The answers are on a scale of 0–10. Promoters, or evangelists as I call them, score 9s and 10s and are typically loyal and enthusiastic customers who are happy to tell their friends about your business. Passives respond with a score of 7 or 8. They are satisfied with your service but not happy enough to be considered promoters. Detractors respond with a score of 0 to 6. These are unhappy customers who are unlikely to buy from you again and may even discourage others from buying from you.

To calculate your final NPS score, just subtract the percentage of detractors from the percentage of promoters. For example, if 5 percent of respondents are detractors, 25 percent are passives, and 70 percent are promoters, your NPS score would be 75-5 = **70**.

The more evangelists we have for our business, the more successful we will be.

The word *evangelize* comes from the Latin *evangelizare*, "to spread or preach the gospel," with the Greek root *euangelizesthai*, which means "bringing good news."[1] The term *evangelism marketing* draws from the religious sense, as consumers are driven by their beliefs in a product or service, which they preach in an attempt to convert others. Evangelism marketing is an advanced form of word-of-mouth marketing in which companies develop customers who believe so strongly in a particular product or service that they freely try to convince others to buy and use it. The customers become voluntary advocates, promoters, actively spreading the word on behalf of your company. The fact that evangelists are not associated with your company make their beliefs perceived by others as credible and trustworthy, and that is the epitome of word-of-mouth advertising.

IN THE TRENCHES
Top Three Ways to Grow Evangelists in Your Business

1.) Knock Their Socks Off

As we learned about word-of-mouth advertising in Chapter 7, you must be extraordinary to be talked about. By creating a remarkable experience, people will remark about your business, but you must first do something astonishingly astounding to remark about.

2.) Ask Them to Refer You and Give Them a Reason

A survey done by Texas Tech University says that 83 percent of your satisfied customers are willing to refer your business, but only 29 percent actually do.[2] Why is that? There are many reasons, but mainly because you did not ask.

---

[1] https://www.etymonline.com/word/evangelist?ref=etymonline_crossreference
[2] https://today.ttu.edu/posts/2018/05/close-referral-gap

3.) Make Your Evangelist Look Good

Once you get a referral from your evangelist, take care of the referred. Call them immediately—do not drop the ball—and make sure they have an excellent experience. You can give the referred a discount or gift with purchase and tell them it's courtesy of the person who referred them (your evangelist). Word will get back to them, and they will be highly incentivized to do it again.

SECTION 3

CHAPTER 13

P.R.O.S.P.E.R. FORMULA

If you narrow down all the possible ways to dramatically increase your net profit, there really are only seven. These seven make up the P.R.O.S.P.E.R. Formula.

Prospecting (Increase)

Ratio of Sales Closed (Increase)

Order Average (Increase)

Sales Frequency (Increase)

Productivity (Increase)

Expenses (Decrease)

Retention (Increase)

Though it is unlikely he said it, Einstein has been attributed as saying, "The law of compounding is the most powerful force in the universe." Well, I am not willing to say it's the most powerful force in the universe, but it is darn close.

With the power of compounding, you only need to do four of the seven ingredients of the P.R.O.S.P.E.R. Formula to double your net bottom line. On average, you will only need to increase (or decrease in the case of expenses) each tactic by 3–7 percent—that is all! That's a powerful formula and certainly doable.

Bestselling author and Wizard of Ads Roy Williams explains compounding this way. "Exponential Little Bits (ELBs): Tiny but relentless changes that compound to make a miracle. The power of an ELB lies not in its size, but in its daily occurrence. For an ELB to work its exponential magic, the little bit must happen every day … every day … Every Day."[3] This is exactly how the P.R.O.S.P.E.R. Formula works. Small but relentless, consistent changes that compound. Each ingredient will increase your profit, but stack them together and you get massive, predictable, exponential, compounding improvement.

According to the Small Business Association (SBA), in 2022, in the U.S. there are 31.7 million small to medium businesses (SMBs). Of those, 81 percent, or 25.7 million, have no employees (termed nonemployers) and 19 percent, or 6 million, have paid employees. The average net profit of SMBs is 7 percent. If your business makes $1,000,000 in gross revenue, the average net profit, after all expenses, is $70,000. That's not a lot for how hard you work. Also, according to the SBA, less than 10 percent of SMBs make over 10 percent net profit! I think that statistic is horrific, and that's why I am on a mission to help double the net profit of 1,000 SMBs, and I am well on my way.

Let us do some math. Let's say your business has gross sales of $1,000,000 and your net bottom line is $70,000. If you increase your prospects by a measly 5 percent, increase your closing ratio by 5 percent, increase your order average by 5 percent, and cut your expenses by 5 percent, you will double your net bottom line to $141,750. Is that not astounding? Obviously, this depends on your average order size and variable expenses, but the P.R.O.S.P.E.R. Formula works for all businesses. Imagine what would happen if you implemented all seven ingredients in the formula! I have put several sample incomes statements from different industries in the appendix where you can see the exact math. You can download the P.R.O.S.P.E.R. Formula spreadsheet at https://prosperoformula.com/resources.

Let us break down each of the seven ingredients in the P.R.O.S.P.E.R. Formula.

---

[3] https://www.mondaymorningmemo.com/newsletters/exponential-little-bits/

CHAPTER 14

(P) PROSPECTING
(Increase Your Prospects
by 5 Percent)

30K FOOT VIEW

Basic sales 101 says you first must have a list of "suspects." Suspects could simply be a database of people who could potentially be your client, customer, or patient. A suspect becomes a prospect when they have been qualified as fitting certain criteria outlined by your company based on the product or service you deliver. A prospect then turns into a lead once they have raised their hand in interest in some way. Online, it's easy to see someone who has shown a bit of interest. They could have simply opened a cold outreach email from you, or clicked on a banner ad, or looked at your social media page, or clicked through to your website, or watched some of your video, or opted in to get more information, or asked a question to your chatbot, or actually called your business. All of these actions would qualify them as a prospect and possibly a lead, and all of them should be followed up with. Your offline marketing should be driving prospects to one of these online conversions so that you can track who is the lead. People who click through your pay-per-click ads skip the prospect stage and should be immediately seen as a hot lead and then followed-up with. They were specifically looking for your product or service. Intrusive marketing, on the other hand, must go through another step of nurturing the prospect. Once someone has raised their hand, we should immediately follow up with them. We could make an offer or nurture the relationship; either way, we should take immediate action. This could simply be a phone call, follow-up email, text message, video, or other content. You can also run retargeting ads that follow them around the web to remind them of your business. I will go into detail on several specific things you could do to increase your prospects. You do not have to do them all, just a few of them because remember, we only need to increase your prospects by 5 percent.

IN THE TRENCHES
Four Ways to Increase Your Prospects

1.) Marketing/Advertising

Marketing is defined as the practice of increasing awareness, consideration, and preference for a product or service through advertising, packaging, placement, pricing, and promotions. Advertising is part of marketing and includes traditional advertising and online marketing. Advertising and marketing are either an expense or an investment (the way you tell the difference is if you made an ROI).

We cover a lot of different forms of marketing in this book. Shockingly, according to a survey done by Outbound Engine in 2019, over 50 percent of all SMB's do not have a marketing and advertising plan. This is amazingly disconcerting to me. How do they expect their business to stay in business, let alone grow? The same survey showed that 54 percent of the businesses surveyed spent less than 5 percent of gross revenues on marketing and advertising. Not surprisingly, of those businesses, less than 50 percent report revenue growth. However, 81 percent of businesses who invested between 5 and 10 percent of annual revenue in marketing said they experienced revenue growth.

2.) Sales

If marketing and advertising is where you get prospects to reach out to you, sales is where you reach out to them. This could be as simple as cold calling with outbound telemarketing or something a little harder like actually pounding the pavement, knocking on doors, and sitting knee-to-knee with a prospect. Other sales channels are tradeshow sales, where you sell from your booth, and virtual sales through webinars, email, chatbots, and websites. All of these are effective when done consistently, and the most successful businesses do them all.

3.) Referrals

Referral marketing is a marketing tactic that makes use of recommendations and word of mouth to grow a business's customer base through the networks of its existing customers. Referrals are an excellent way to increase your prospects. The referral is one key foundational element to any good sales strategy, and learning how to get referrals is incredibly important. We talked a little about referrals in Chapter 12, "Evangelize."

At its core, referral marketing is about enabling and incentivizing your existing customer base to encourage their friends and family to come and try your product or service for the first time.

According to a survey undertaken by independent research company Opinion Matters, leads coming from referrals enjoy a 30 percent higher conversion rate compared to those coming from other marketing channels. They also found that referred customers are 18 percent more loyal, have a 16 percent higher lifetime value rate, and spend 13 percent more than their non-referred counterparts.

To increase your referrals, you must have a consistent quantifiable referral program. Sadly, less than 30 percent of SMBs have a structured referral program. Referrals programs don't have to be complicated. Start with the 20 percent who send you 80 percent of your referrals. Set up a program that will incentivize them to send you even more referrals. Then market your referral program to all your customers, past and present. There are several excellent apps and software that can help you organize and systematize a referral program. Extole.com, ReferralCandy.com, Friendbuy.com, and helloreferrals.com are a few great ones.

4.) Joint Ventures Partners

Another terrific way to bring in more prospects is Joint Ventures (JV) Partners. We talked about this in Chapter 10, "TRY."

The number of consistent prospects that you bring into your business is critical to its success. I need you to increase it by 5 percent.

CHAPTER 15

(R) RATIO OF
SALES CLOSED
(Increase Your Closing
Ratio by 5 Percent)

30K FOOT VIEW

By the end of my freshman year in college, my parents made it clear that I would have to get a job because they were cutting me off. Luckily for me, I had the gift of gab and quickly landed a prestigious position as a customer service representative, or CSR, better known as a telemarketer. I had one mission only: to sell the Allstate Deluxe Motor Club, which was like AAA Motor Club, but better. After my two-day training intensive, I was strapped into a cubicle and dialing for dollars.

Once I got a live human on the phone, I was to quickly go into reading the automatized spiel off the computer monitor. The pitch was packed with features and benefits. If someone threw us an objection, we had at our fingertips a rebuttal for every single one of them. We would simply rebuke that objection and then move back into the spiel.

Then, just like clockwork, we would get another objection and we would punch the button, switch gears, handle the objection, and then move on to the close. We were not allowed to let them go until we got two no's or a hang-up. The odds of them saying yes were less than 2 percent.

I know what some of you are thinking: you would rather pour Tabasco sauce in your eye and headbutt a porcupine than be a telemarketer. Well, from experience, it is about the same amount of pain.

I only worked there about a year and a half before I moved into radio, but it has been the crux of my sales success my entire life. Let me break down the exact steps to increasing your closing ratio that I learned from my CSR days.

IN THE TRENCHES
Eight Ways to Increase Your Closing Ratio

1.) Accurately Qualify Your Prospects

We already talked about this in the previous chapter. Much of the real work in closing a sale is actually done in preliminary research where you qualify your prospect and determine whether or not they stand to benefit from your solution. If your prospect does not fit your ideal customer profile, then the effort is basically futile, and you are wasting your time (and theirs) pursuing them.

When I was in telemarketing, our lists would come from Sears or Discover Card holders. They would segment them by location and age. One time, unbeknownst to us CSRs we started calling from a list of people who were under the age of 50. One of the main benefits of the Deluxe Motor Club was huge senior citizen discounts on hotels and motels. As you might have guessed, we got massacred (except I am proud to say that I was the only one to make a sale). The problem was clear: we were not calling qualified prospects.

2.) Bond

In Chapter 8: "Like," we discussed the four types of people and how to bond with those people. Bonding is critical to closing sales whether it's in five minutes for the Deluxe Motor Club or a five-million-dollar piece of equipment that takes up to two years to close. People do business with people they know, like, and trust. It only took me a week or two in my CSR career to learn that the standard scripts basically sucked, so I started experimenting with my own script. At first the quality assurance gals were all over me, telling me to stick to the script. But I started making sales, lots of them. In fact, ultimately, I broke every record in the company. Eventually, headquarters recruited me to help them write the new scripts. What was my secret? Bonding. That's it. The only thing I changed was that I personalized every call. I started by just simply asking them how they were doing. This was supposedly a big no-no. We were to jump right into to the spiel before they could say "I'm not interested." I took the opposite route. I wanted to bond with these people first. I would try to find some common ground. If I heard a dog in the background, I ask what kind of dog it was. People love to talk about their pets. If they were from Texas, I would say, "How about them Cowboys?" or from Alabama, "Roll Tide." I did not let things get too off track; they all knew that I was calling to pitch them something, but most of them respected that I took a moment to bond. Once we bonded, I would say, "Look, I know you are busy, so I'll get straight to the point," and because we'd bonded, 90 percent of them let me completely finish my spiel. This was the secret to closing more deals.

3.) Connect the Application (Not Just Your Product or Service Features and Benefits)

The secret to my success as a telemarketer was that I just had to get them to listen to the entire pitch. The Deluxe Motor Club was a great solution to common problems that we all ran into back then. It was truly a great deal, especially if they compared it to the AAA Motor Club. It had more benefits, better benefits, and it was cheaper. If you just took advantage of the hotel discounts, it paid for itself. But it also included free towing, tire changes, jump starts, gas delivery, and lock out service. It was pretty much guaranteed you would need a few of those things every year and it sucked when you had to pay out of pocket for them; but not with the Deluxe

Motor Club. We call that a no-brainer. Your product or service should be a no-brainer as well.

As Zig Ziglar used to say, "The most popular radio station in the world is WIIFM, What's In It For Me?" You will dramatically increase your closing ratio if you connect the dots that your product or service is the solution to the prospect's problem. This is one step past the classic sales training of "features and benefits." I call it "features, benefits to application." For example, let us look at a home security company that sells security cameras, specifically the fictitious **Acme 990.**

Acme 990, All-in-One Security Camera:
The Features:

Weatherproof, ultrahigh definition camera with a wide-angle lens, night vision, pan-tilt controls and zoom up to 30X, two-way audio, and advanced motion sensor.

The Benefits:

This ultrahigh definition camera with night vision allows you to see vivid details even in bright sunlight or complete darkness. You will be able to adjust the angle and zoom lens from your smartphone anywhere, putting you in control of your security. This camera is weather and waterproof rated, surviving temperatures between -40 degrees and 158 degrees Fahrenheit. The advanced motion sensor will trigger the camera to record video when motion is detected, but if you choose, it will only alert you when it's confirmed motion from a human. The two-way audio allows you to speak with (and listen to) whomever is outside.

Application:

If you have ever had a package stolen from your porch or had a car broken into while parked in your driveway, there is a good chance that the perpetrator was long gone before you even found out you had been victimized. There is an even better chance that you will never know who committed the deed. If this sounds familiar, it is time to invest in the Acme 990 all-in-one premier outdoor security camera. You will never again worry about catching the thief or other unwanted visitors. Once you get an alert that someone is on your property, you can quickly distinguish if it is a friend or foe by zooming in on their face even if it is pitch-dark. If it is foe, you can talk to the person, sound an alarm and/or dispatch police, while it is being recorded in ultrahigh definition for evidence for the police.

Hopefully, my security camera example clarifies why you must emotionally tie your product or service to the prospect. Just in case, another feature versus benefit example is a drill. They say no one wants a drill; they buy a drill because they need a hole. To take that one step further to the "application" stage, no one wants a drill or a hole; they want a picture hung on a wall, that's the application. If you want to close more sales, be sure and connect how your product or service directly applies to your prospect. In the end, consumers only care about what's in it for them.

4.) Create Urgency and Scarcity

Urgency is a time-based strategy, making customers develop a fear of missing out (FOMO), which compels them to buy within the limited time constraints. Scarcity is where your prospect perceives that there's a limited supply. Both are certainly motivators for a prospect to buy now. It helps move the sales cycle along and forces a decision. If you look closely, urgency and scarcity is used by all major brands. Amazon is famous for Cyber Monday sales or Prime Day, with countdown timers, which forces urgency. They also always put a limited supply, with the big bold words "Only x number available." This is scarcity. You can do similar things in your business, and it will increase your closing ratio.

5.) Overcome Their Objections and Concerns

Whether it's on the phone, in person, or online, you must expect some friction in the sales cycle. Rarely does a prospect say, "Ok, here's my money." Knowing this, you should be prepared to address every possible objection. Essentially, all objections fall into five distinct categories.

Categories of Objections and How to Overcome Them

Monetary Objections

Obviously, price objections are one of the most common objections in any sales cycle. Fortunately, price is one of the easiest objections to overcome. "It's too expensive," "That's not in the budget," or "I can get this cheaper somewhere else" are all simply saying they do not see commensurate value. Value is simply defined as how much the prospects perceive your products or services to be worth—their anticipated price that's in their head—against how much the product or service actually costs. It is imperative that your customers think your products or services hold greater value than your price or no one will buy. It's our job as marketers and business owners to make it a no-brainer. The only two ways to increase value, either drop the price, which I don't recommend, or increase the perceived value, which you can easily do through marketing.

Time-Related Objections

You have probably heard one of these objections: "We're too busy right now," "I have too much going on," "Call me back in x months." In a similar fashion to money-related objections, time-related sales objections revolve around a lack of resources—whether actual or perceived. It comes down to how much time and energy it will take to change. Remember, Anthony Robbins says something along these lines: Until the pain of staying the same is more than the pain of change, people won't change. To overcome this objection, you must either eliminate the pain of change or exacerbate the pain of staying the same, or both.

Complacency or Contentment?

You might often hear such prospects raise objections like "We already use (X product/service); it would be a huge pain to switch over," or "I am okay with my current setup." Overcoming this objection is done in the same way as for the time-related objection. You must either eliminate the pain of change or exacerbate the pain of staying the same, or both.

Lacks Authority to Make a Decision

Another common sales objection you are likely to encounter, whether in the B2B or B2C realm, is one in which an individual claims to not have the authority to make a purchasing decision. A couple of examples: "My boss is in charge of that," and "I need to check with my wife/husband." The best time to learn this is before you spend a bunch of time pitching your goods and services to people who cannot say yes. Always ask in advance, "Who else needs to be in this meeting?" The other issue is if they plan on explaining your product or service to their spouse or boss or whomever, there is not an inkling of a chance they will pitch your product or service as well as you. It's okay if all the decision makers were not in the room when you gave the pitch. Sometimes you must sell the gatekeeper first before they let you get to the decision maker. If they see immense value in your product or service, they will help you set up another appointment with the missing decision makers.

Blow Offs

There is always the possibility that a given prospect simply refuses to give you a real objection. It will be generic, like "I'm not interested," "Sure, send me some info and I will get back to you," or the one I use to get telemarketers off the phone, "We will not be doing that." These are all blow offs and are hard to overcome. The best you can do is ask a question that may lead you to a real objection. I will usually switch gears and ask a very pointed question about their pain, maybe something about their competitors. Sometimes that gets them to open up.

6.) Ask for the Sale

It is absolutely perplexing to me how many people pitch their product or service and don't ask for the sale. When I was the General Sales Manager for a radio station, many times I would go with my sales staff to pitch the marketing package. They would do an excellent job of qualifying the prospect, they bonded with them, and they would pitch the benefits and application to the business owner. They would amplify the urgency and overcome all their objections. Then they would stand up and hold out their hand and say, "Let me know if you have any more questions." I would usually just sit in my chair and not get up. Confused, they would say, "Let's go." I would smile and say, "You have not asked for the order." The business owner always laughed because I was right and a good portion of the time, they ended up signing the proposal on the spot because we asked. Always ask for the sale. They will either sign it or tell you another objection.

7.) Have a Guarantee or Warranty

The guarantee serves as a promise made by the manufacturer or business to the buyer, that in case the product or service is below the advertised value, it will be repaired, replaced, or the money deposited will be refunded.

A warranty is a written assurance about a tangible product. It specifies that the product is up to advertised standards in quality and performance and is true and genuine, but if it is not, it will be repaired, replaced, or the money will be refunded.

Your business should definitely have a guarantee and also a warranty if you sell physical products. This is the easiest form of risk reversal in marketing and takes away some of the fear and anxiety of buying your product or service.

By having a good, legitimate guarantee, you are forcing your business to put the customer first and setting a bar for minimum standards.

What makes a good guarantee and warranty?

a. It is unconditional. A guarantee loses power in direct proportion to the number of conditions it contains.

b. It is easy to understand and communicate.

c. It is quick, easy, and painless to invoke and collect.

In May of 2007, Hyundai issued a press release that massively shook up the auto industry. Fountain Valley-based Hyundai Motor America launched the industry's most generous warranty program on earth. Bumper-to-bumper coverage and free roadside assistance for five years or 60,000 miles, with coverage of the powertrain components—engine and transmission—extended to 10 years and 100,000 miles.

Since announcing the warranty, Hyundai sales in the U.S. have skyrocketed by more than 70 percent and the company has been able to cut back dramatically on discounting and incentive programs.

In the P.R.O.S.P.E.R. Formula coaching program, our guarantee is 30-day unconditional. I will refund your money no matter what, if you do not like me, my jokes, or whatever. We also have 365 conditional—if you have implemented the formula and have not doubled your net profit, I will work with you for free until you do.

If you have a great guarantee or warranty, your closing ratio will certainly go up.

8.) Follow-up

In September of 2020, my house took a direct hit from hurricane Sally. We had 17 trees fall, none on our house thankfully, but we did lose a lot of shingles, some windows were damaged, our pool and well got damaged, and so on. Once we filed an insurance claim, I had five different contractors come out to give me a quote for the various items. They took the time to set an appointment, come to my house, assess the damage, and write a proposal. The most baffling thing is it has been over two years later and not one of them has followed up with me.

If a prospective client has metaphorically raised their hand that they are interested in your product or service and you went out of your way to give them a proposal, you have earned the right to follow up, and you absolutely should.

On large-ticket items, one-call closes rarely exist anymore. According to the 2021 sales statistics by HubSpot, 48 percent of businesses never follow up at all. Let me yell that statistic at you: ALMOST 50 PERCENT OF BUSINESSES NEVER FOLLOW UP AT ALL. Only 44 percent of businesses follow up once, and less than 8 percent follow up more than once. Sixty percent of customers say no four times before saying yes. But in a lot of cases, they never said "No," they just said "Not now."

Another interesting stat from the study shows that following up with web leads within five minutes makes you nine times more likely to engage with them. But less than 5 percent do it.

If you accurately qualify your prospects, bond with them, connect the dots in how it applies to them, create urgency and scarcity, master handling objections, strategically and consistently ask for the sale, and follow up, it is absolutely guaranteed your closing ratio will go up considerably. The good news is we only need your closing ratio to go up by 5 percent.

CHAPTER 16

(O) ORDER AVERAGE
(Increase Your Average Order by 5 Percent)

30K FOOT VIEW

O ne of the key performance indicators (KPIs) you should calculate every single month is your order average. You simply take the total number of sales divided by total income. This is a vital metric you must know to have a successful business. If you want to get fancy, and you can remember pre-algebra, you can calculate the three measures of central tendency:

- **Mean:** the average value of all orders (what we traditionally call Order Average or Average Order). This is all you need in business if you don't have any extremes.
- **Mode:** the most frequently occurring order value, the most common order size. This isn't helpful for small businesses, too much wiggle room.
- **Median:** The median is the middle-of-the-road number. Half of the people are above the median and half are below the median. (In the U.S., it is literally the middle of the road; a median is the middle of the highway. This is especially useful for those businesses

that have extremes. When my wife and I first bought the award shop, I would simply just calculate the mean. But I quickly realized my numbers were overtly skewed. On the low end, I had dozens of orders that had zero dollars. They were donations to charities or local high schools. On the high end, a few times a year we would sell a 70-foot flagpole for $10,000. These extremes really messed with my average. So, in my case, it would be best to calculate the median. However, I quickly found out it was easier to simply take out both extremes and then just calculate the mean.

I do not particularly care which way you calculate your order average, as long as it's consistent. Now that you have your order average, let's talk about a few ways to raise it by 5 percent.

IN THE TRENCHES
Five Ways to Increase Your Order Average

1.) Raise Your Prices

By far, the simplest and easiest thing you can do to raise your order average is raise your prices across the board. I would argue that 95 percent of all SMBs can raise their prices by 3 percent and not lose a single customer. A survey done by Emplifi confirms that at least 65 percent of U.S. consumers would happily pay 5 percent more for products if they knew they would receive outstanding customer service.

Economists use a measurement called price elasticity to assess the change in consumer demand as a result of a change in a good or service's price. Most local small businesses' prices are inelastic, meaning the demand will not drop if you raise your price. The reason is because most of your customers are not buying from you because of price. They buy because they know, like, and trust you. If you own a hair salon and your average order is $60, a price increase to $63 is almost unnoticeable, and your customer certainly will not go down the street and risk using a new stylist over $3. If you own an auto repair shop and you raise your shop hour rate from $85 to $89.25, if they know, like, and trust you, not one customer would risk trying a new mechanic over $4.25 per hour. If you have a business that has monthly recurring revenue, you can raise your prices 10 to 20 percent for new clients and grandfather in your current clients or maybe only raise them a little. The goal is to average a 5 percent increase overall.

I do understand that, with the internet at our thumb tips, certain products and services have been turned into a commodity and it is easier than ever to compare prices and buy somewhere else. If you have commodity type of goods or services in your business, the goal would be to achieve a meaningful difference from any others that are available. In Chapter 8: Like, we discussed six distinct reasons people choose a business; only one was price. Use one or more of the other five to compete on something other than price. If you cannot make a compelling argument about why you differ, then you probably can't raise your price. Do not worry, if this is the case, there are four other ways to increase your order average by 5 percent.

Presentation

This is a tactical way to increase your prices. Last summer I went to the behemoth Bass Pro Shop in downtown Memphis, Tennessee. Upstairs in their game calls section they have a luxurious private room encased in glass that has a duck call sitting on a black pedestal with a spotlight gloriously shining down on it. It's the Tim Grounds Harley Pear Triple Crown Goose Call, and it costs $199.99. That's one heck of a markup for what amounts to a few dollars in metal and plastic parts. The average duck call is under $20. There is no conceivable way they could sell that duck call for two hundred dollars if it were just hanging on a hook next to the other duck calls. The key is presentation.

There is a new franchise called Crumbl Cookies, and they sell very high-end cookies that are packaged in a nice pink box. The only way you can sell a cookie for an average of over $3.65 each is by marketing and packaging. Speaking of boxes, probably the most famous one is Tiffany

& Co.'s simple light blue box tied with a white ribbon. It has become an international symbol of luxury and sophistication. Even though the packaging adds a little more expense, it is easy to tack on 20 to 100 percent more to the price.

2.) Upsell

By all accounts, McDonald's is attributed to inventing the upsell. They have been asking, "Do you want fries with that?" for over 60 years. That one simple question that takes less than three seconds to ask, has been estimated to have increased McDonald's average order by over 5 to 7 percent almost overnight. Every single business should be trying to upsell every single customer.

Grocery stores do it with impulse items at the checkout counter. Car dealerships upsell by adding on warranties, floor mats, gold emblems, and so on. BMW is now upselling their mobile app ConnectedDrive for around $15 a month, which will add millions to their bottom line. Dentists upsell with teeth whitening or gold crowns. E-commerce stores upsell by offering additional items that go with the item you are looking to buy. Cross-fit gym memberships are sold with private coaching and supplements.

If you have a home services company, your techs should be saying "While I'm here, would you like me to ..." then offer whatever else you do, "flush your hot water heater, clean out your dryer vent, install new flushing mechanisms on your toilet." What can you offer as an upsell that will increase your average order?

One of our security alarm clients simply added three upsell questions on the order form and made every customer opt out by checking the box that they do not want it. These are things like warranties on the cameras and unlimited data storage and mobile app upgrades. The majority of his customers keep all three items, which added over 15 percent to his average monthly recurring revenue.

All businesses should be offering an upsell.

3.) Slack Adjuster

A slack adjuster is a "super upsell." They cost 10 to 100 times more than the core offering. The Pareto Principle (80/20 rule) tells us that if you had 1,000 customers who bought your core offer at $5, then roughly 200 (20%) of your customers would buy something for $50. But then you have the 20% of those people (20% of the 20% or 4% of the total), 40 people would be willing to buy something for $500. Most businesses would stop there, but eight (.8% of your total customers) would be willing to buy something for $5,000. I know you are thinking this is absolutely absurd, but every extraordinarily successful business understands this and has an offer just for those people.

For example, Starbucks sometimes will sell a $3,000 espresso machine in their stores. They don't sell a lot of them, but it is a huge profit boost and average order boost when they do. Disney has a World of Dreams VIP Tour with club level Fast Passes that sells for over $12,000 a day, not including lodging. The average Rolex watch sells for about $12,000, but of course they understand what a slack adjuster is, and if you are the 20 percent of the 20 percent, you can buy the run-of-the-mill Rolex Datejust Submariner for a measly $194,599, but for the .8%, you can buy the Rolex Cosmograph Daytona Everose Rainbow Watch, which is for sale right now for $674,000, and yes, they have sold more than a few of them.

4.) Bundles/Packages/Kits

The toothpaste and deodorant industry ran out of unique ways to sell their items, so they started just selling two tubes packaged together. This immediately increased their average order. Bundling and packages are great because it's hard to price shop. In my award shop, we give away a free coach's plaque with every team order of trophies over ten. The prices of our trophies are much higher than our competitors', but when you bundle them with a plaque, it's hard to compare. What usually happens is they buy a second plaque for the assistant coach.

5.) **Bonus or Discount after Threshold**

Many e-commerce stores offer free shipping once you hit a price threshold. They set the threshold a little higher than their average order. For instance, if their average order is $42, they will advertise free shipping with orders over $50. This will incentivize shoppers to put one more thing in their cart to hit the threshold. In your business, you could offer a gift with purchase or some other bonus once they hit a certain price point above your average.

Of course, you need to do the math and make sure your net profit is higher after you subtract the cost of the bonus.

You can also increase your average order with volume discounts. In the screen-printing business, it's a huge pain to set up the press for a multi-color shirt. You must make the negatives, then burn the screens, register the screens, set up the ink at each station, and so on. The majority of your time is in the setup, (and clean up). It may take you an hour to make 48 shirts. But it would only take you an hour and a half to make 244 shirts. Because of the economies of scale, you can offer large volume discounts to entice your customer to buy more. Maybe this can apply to your business to increase your average order.

You can easily implement some of these tactics in your business to increase your average order. The amazing thing is all the increase goes straight to your bottom line. Our Poop Emoji Plumbing business example in the appendix of this book has gross sales of one million dollars. If you raise the average order by 5 percent, you will add $50,000 to your net profit. If your total net profit was the average of 10 percent before ($100,000), by doing just this one tactic from the P.R.O.S.P.E.R. Formula, you just increased your net profit by 50 percent!

CHAPTER 17

(S) SALES FREQUENCY
(Increase Your Frequency of Sales by 5 Percent)

30K FOOT VIEW

Any business broker will tell you that the businesses that sell for the highest multiple are the ones that have monthly recurring revenue, especially ones with long-term contracts. The reason is consistency and predictability. Monthly recurring revenue is the ultimate goal, but even if you can increase your average sales frequency just a fraction more, it will dramatically increase your bottom line, plus increase the overall value of your business.

One example is how the entire auto industry changed the game in 1993 when they started pushing customers to lease vehicles instead of buying them. This effectively moved the customers from buying cars every five to seven years to every three years, because most leases at the time were for three years. Their bottom line skyrocketed because they moved up the buying process by years (plus they could add crazy undisclosed fees on a lease).

Another splendid example of increasing the frequency of sales is back in 2018, Adobe, Inc., took a huge risk and forced its customers to move over to a monthly or annual subscription model. Their stock jumped 29.10

percent for that year and continues a steep climb. At the end of 2021, ADBE is now up over 345 percent from January 2018. Before the change, their customers would buy only every third or fourth updated version of the software on average, and which new version they would buy was unpredictable. But by forcing the subscription program, they get predictable, consistent income.

According to the American Dental Association, 52.3 percent of adults reported that they had visited the dentist every six months during the last few years, 15.4 percent reported once per year, and 11.0 percent reported once every two to three years. More than one in five (21.3 percent) reported that they had not visited the dentist in the last few years. So, let us do some math on a hypothetical dentist. One thousand patients total, 52 percent come twice a year, 15 percent come once per year, and let's average that 11 percent of the patients come every two years and 22 percent every four years. What if we used software that nurtures, reminds, and automatically follows up with the patient and will help the dentist get the patients to come in more frequently and not miss their scheduled appointments. What if we could get 15 percent of the non-frequent patients, the 11 percent and the 22 percent, to come in once a year? How many more appointments would the practice have this year? Well, if we do the math, 11 percent is 110 patients, and 22 percent is 220 patients. Three hundred thirty total patients, in which we persuaded 15 percent of them to come in at least once per year. That's 50 more appointments per year. We just raised our sales frequency by 5 percent.

IN THE TRENCHES
Five Ways to Increase Your Sales Frequency

1.) Monthly Membership/ Monthly
Recurring Revenue (MRR)

The car wash industry has dramatically increased the average monthly spend of a customer by offering unlimited washes for something like $34 a month, which was almost 20 percent higher than their previous monthly average per customer. This has been a game changer for the industry.

If you are sitting there thinking this will never work for your industry, I would like to implore you that there is probably a way to get your customers on a continuity program. Coffee, wine, vitamins, pet food, pet toys, makeup, socks, razors, and even fishing gear all have phenomenally successful monthly membership programs where they automatically send you your order each month. On a local level, you can now buy memberships to bars and nightclubs, brew pubs, bowling alleys, ice cream shops, movie theaters, hair salons, car washes, gyms, HVAC maintenance, oil changes and yes, gas stations. Your business too can implement a monthly recurring sales program.

2.) VIP Programs

In exchange for a small up-front monthly, quarterly, or annual fee, you can immediately open up your VIP customers to some exclusive benefits and discounts. Amazon Prime is considered the best VIP program ever contrived, with around 82 percent of their customers (over 200 million) opting in. It's incalculable how much more money they have brought in because of their VIP program. You can sell a VIP program at your local business and offer things like skip the line, free valet parking, free dessert, extra shot of espresso, 24-hour emergency service for free, and so on.

3.) Loyalty Programs

Loyalty programs are earned over time and have a couple different forms. One way is to incorporate point accumulation like sticker or punch card programs. The other way is tiered purchase programs, which is based on expenditure rather than just quantity.

4.) Bounce Back/Exit Offers

This is where you entice your customer to come back sooner than they normally would. Kohl's has mastered this with Kohl's Cash. Shop during a

Kohl's Cash earn period and get $10 Kohl's Cash for every $50 you spend. Redemption is a little complicated to me and it varies. Essentially you get a five-to-nine-day period in which to redeem the coupon within the next 30 days. This would be easy to implement in retail shops like local clothing stores, local coffee shops, hair and nail salons, chiropractors, massages therapists, spas, pool supplies, and the like.

5.) Birthday/Anniversary Coupon

This is one of most impactful and easiest tactics you can do to get your customer to come in more frequently, at least one more time per year, plus everyone likes to get birthday gifts.

CHAPTER 18

(P) PRODUCTIVITY
(Increase Your Productivity by 5 Percent)

30K FOOT VIEW

In my marketing agency, one of our seven core values is "productivity, not just activity." Productivity, by definition, produces a verifiable result. Not all activity actually produces a result. At the end of the day when you lay your head on your pillow, do not ask yourself, "How hard did I work today?" Ask yourself, "What results did I get today?" This is a vastly different question. Results are often harsh but always fair.

The Japanese have a term, *kaizen*, meaning change for the better or continuous improvement. It is a business philosophy that continuously improves operations, systems, and processes and involves all employees. Kaizen sees improvement in productivity as a gradual and methodical process. I think this is an excellent philosophy. It implies that you will never arrive, you must always continue to improve.

In his 1954 book *The Practice of Management*, Peter Drucker said, "What gets measured gets managed." Drucker also said, "You can't manage what you can't measure," and "What gets measured gets improved." All these statements are absolutely true. Unfortunately, less than 30 percent of all small businesses consistently measure their productivity.

Productivity defined is the efficiency of production of goods or services expressed by some measure, either quantity, quality, or time.

So basically, if you can measure the quantity output or if you can measure the quality of the output out or if you can measure how much time it takes to produce the output, you can measure productivity. Since you can measure it, you can manage it and improve it.

Some businesses seem nebulous when it comes to productivity. For instance, on the surface, how can a law firm be more efficient? Or an accountant? I am here to tell you there is always a way to increase productivity in every industry, in every niche.

It's easy to measure the efficiency of a production line. Massive movements for process improvements have swept the world like Six Sigma, Lean manufacturing, Agile, and Total Quality Management (TQM).

The Four Main Process Improvement (Productivity) Methodologies

1.) Six Sigma

A data-driven approach to reduce defects to improve an organization's performance. The most popular Six Sigma method is the DMAIC.

Define the opportunity for improvement (project goal)

Measure the performance of your existing process

Analyze the process to find any defects and their root causes

Improve the process by addressing the root causes you found

Control the improved process and future process performance to correct any deviations before they result in defects

2.) Lean Manufacturing

A systematic process to minimize waste without sacrificing productivity.

The seven lean principles are:

1. Eliminate waste
2. Build quality in
3. Create knowledge
4. Defer commitment
5. Deliver fast
6. Respect people
7. Optimize the whole

3.) Agile Manufacturing

Strives to deliver more usable and useful products and services by staying nimble and by focusing on customer success.

Individuals and interactions over processes and tools.

Working software over comprehensive documentation.

Customer collaboration over contract negotiation.

Responding to change over following a plan.

4.) Total Quality Management (TQM)

An organization-wide effort focused on continuous improvement to improve customer quality. They do this by implementing PDCA cycles (Plan, Do, Check, Act).

Organizations should follow a strategic and systematic approach to achieve their goals.

Customers determine the level of quality.

All employees work toward common goals. Effective communication and training ensure that everyone understands the definition of quality and strives to achieve it.

Organizations should define the required steps of any process and monitor performance to detect any deviations. They should continually look for ways to be more effective and more competitive.

How do these apply to your business? I do not think it's necessary to hire a productivity consultant who specializes in one of these unless you think it would dramatically change your business. In most cases, I believe you could easily figure out where your business is not efficient. In fact, most of the time it's glaringly obvious. Remember, we only need to increase your productivity by 5 percent for the P.R.O.S.P.E.R. Formula.

IN THE TRENCHES
Four Ways to Increase Productivity in Your Business

1.) Hawthorne Effect

The Hawthorne effect is a type of reactivity in which individuals modify an aspect of their behavior in response to their awareness of being observed.

The term was coined during research experiments on lighting at Western Electric's factory in the Hawthorne suburb of Chicago in the early 1930s. The study was to determine if increasing or decreasing the amount of light would have an effect on productivity. What the studies found was that almost all productivity went up, even when subjected to extremes on both ends of the spectrum. They studied productivity in extreme bright lights down to the levels of candlelight, and in both situations, productivity increased. The researchers concluded that workers were responding to the increased attention from managers and researchers. This suggested that productivity increased due to attention and not because of changes in the experimental variables.

What we can learn from this is we should give our employees more attention. I like to say, "Keep your thumb on them." You can also simply set up cameras in the work area, and productivity will go up.

That same thing applies when you start tracking stats. While a piñata game is best played with a blindfold, business isn't. Remember, what gets measured gets improved.

In his book *Traction: Get a Grip on Your Business*, Gino Wickman makes a very persuasive argument that all jobs should have a number. Meaning everyone is accountable to some stat. Gino gives very compelling reasons to track the numbers. Here are a few.

- Numbers cut through murky subjective communication between manager and direct reports
- Numbers create accountability
- Numbers create clarity and commitment
- Accountable people appreciate numbers
- Numbers create competition
- Numbers produce results
- Numbers create teamwork
- You solve problems faster
- Tracking numbers increases productivity

2.) Level 10 Meetings

Once again, Gino Wickman is spot on. He says we should have a goal that all our meetings are productive, or we should not have them. He calls them level 10 meetings, which implies that the meeting was a 10 out 10 for productivity. Not 4 or 7 … a 10. The only way to make your meetings level 10 is to have a very specific strategic plan with a purpose for each minute in the meeting.

Here are some guidelines to help make your meetings more productive.

- Always start on time and end on time. There is nothing worse than not knowing how long a meeting is going to be. The least productive time in any meeting is the five minutes before everyone thinks the meeting is going to be over. If you go over the allotted time, people can only think about two things: one, when is this going to finally be over? And two, their bitterness for you not respecting their time.

The second least productive time in any meeting is the first five minutes. With staff meetings, never wait until everyone is in the room or on the call before you get started. As author Eric Jerome Dickey says, "Early is on time, on time is late, and late is unacceptable!" Starting late is disrespectful of those who showed up on time and trains everyone that it's okay to be late. It won't take more than two meetings starting on time before everyone gets the message not to be late.

- Always have an agenda. These can be emailed ahead of time, that way your staff can show up prepared for what will be discussed. If you have a weekly meeting and the agenda is the same every week, make sure you stick to that agenda.
- Start the meeting with good news and end the meeting with good news. Ask if anyone has any success stories either personal or in business. I like to give accolades, awards, and rewards in my weekly and monthly meetings. It does not have to be extravagant; compliments in front of peers go a long way and it quickly sets a positive tone for the meeting. Money and awards are even better.

When I was in the corporate world, I sat in many mundane meetings that took out all human elements. Sometimes we can get so robotic and talk about numbers, issues, policies, and procedures, but we never talked about the human sitting across the conference table. This is time well spent and should only take about five or ten minutes, but it will bring back huge dividends.

- At the core of your agenda, you need to have some reporting. It should be the main KPIs (key performance indicators) you are tracking for each area of your business.
- After you report your numbers and see how each area is progressing, you need to have time for discussion on issues, problems, and goals.

The core of my weekly meetings follows a powerful spreadsheet that was given to me by my friend and bestselling author, Dr. Jim Harris. He called it the D3 tracking sheet. Here's what the Ds mean:

Done: What have you finished the past week, or month?
Doing: What are you working on now?
Do: What will you do by the next meeting?

My business partner and I modified it to the D7 tracking sheet and added these Ds:

Defer: What are you deferring until a later date?
Delete: What are you taking off your list or what are you going to stop doing?
Discussion: What do you want to discuss with the group and get some feedback on?
Decision: What needs to be decided on? Usually, it's the answer to the discussion we just had.

This keeps everyone on track and makes it extremely easy for me to hold everyone accountable. At each meeting, I simply parrot back what they told me they were going to do and ask if they did them.

In most cases, I find that if you just tighten up your meetings and follow this format, you can dramatically increase the productivity of the entire company without doing anything else.

3.) **Time-Blocking**

Having a colleague pop their head into your office to chat may seem innocuous, but even brief interruptions stop your flow. There have been dozens of high-profile studies showing that interruptions in workflow can take 15–25 minutes to get back in the groove again.

A University of California study found that after each interruption, it takes over 23 minutes to refocus.[4] Even worse, if the interruption takes you in a different direction for a brief period, this multitasking can deplete your brainpower to the equivalent of dropping ten IQ points. Ouch! Some of us cannot spare ten IQ points.

Studies show that the average worker is astonishingly interrupted somewhere between four and twelve times every hour. That's one interruption every 15 minutes, in the best-case scenario. These stats seem ridiculous but when you consider all the possible distractions, from coworkers stopping by, phone calls, texts, emails, app notifications, and chat messages, it's obviously a very realistic number and a huge productivity issue.

The solution is time-blocking. Experts say 50- to 90-minute time blocks with 10-minute breaks are ideal for mass productivity. I like to schedule three, 50-minute time blocks a day where I close my office door, shut down email, and get to work. My staff has learned that all issues can wait until my door is open.

To help with coworker interruptions, you can make little "IN FLOW, DO NOT DISTURB" signs that they can post in their cubicle. Or make specific hours when no one can talk or get out of their chair. They must focus for a full hour.

If you have a service business, you can block specific times where there are no appointments where you can work "ON" the business.

---

[4] "Gloria Mark, a professor of informatics at the University of California, Irvine, who studies digital distraction" as referenced in an article by Rachel Emma Silverman, "Workplace Distractions: Here's Why You Won't Finish This Article," *Wall Street Journal* (Updated Dec. 11, 2012) https://www.wsj.com/articles/SB10001424127887324339204578173252223022388

4.) Standard Operating Procedures (SOPs)

What Is an SOP?

In short, this is a step-by-step list of the procedures on exactly how your company does this one single task. SOPs systematize repeated tasks and mostly eliminate making the same mistakes over and over, and they cut down the learning curve when transitioning the responsibility from one employee to another. SOPs should be fluid and adjust with changing times but rigid enough not to change just for change's sake. SOPs will dramatically increase your productivity.

What Should Be in the SOP?

Basic high-level overview of the task. Explanations of the specific goal you are trying to achieve. Who is responsible for getting it done? Then the specific steps of completing task successfully, and the pitfalls to look out for.

When Should You Create the SOP?

Anytime you must do something more than twice.

Who Should Create the SOP?

Whoever is doing the task repeatedly. All others can chime in and add details.

Where Should the SOP Be?

Anywhere and everywhere that will get used. In my award shop, we print and laminate the procedures and post them at the station where it will be used. In my agency, we created an internal wiki that houses all the SOPs and is searchable and editable by everyone.

The productivity ingredient in the P.R.O.S.P.E.R. Formula is the hardest one to enumerate. I think we can all agree that if we increase our productivity by at least 5 percent, it will most definitely show up in our bottom line.

CHAPTER 19

(E) EXPENSES
(Decrease Your Expenses by 5 Percent)

30K FOOT VIEW

E xpenses are the only part of the P.R.O.S.P.E.R. Formula we decrease. A quick vendor audit will always reveal frivolous spending. In our poop emoji plumbing example in the appendix of this book, if we cut the just the variable and fixed expenses by only 5 percent, that equates to over fifty thousand dollars net profit with just this one ingredient of the formula! The good news is the average SMB has over 10 percent fluff in their expenditures that can be cut, even when they think they are running lean. We only need to find 5 percent.

Fortunately for us, all accounting software helps us see exactly what's going on with our expenses. Just to keep things simple, we need to look at our expenses in two categories.

1.) Fixed Expenses

These are expenses that you can expect to stay the same even though you may sell more. Some of these items are rent/mortgage, salaries, utilities, repairs & maintenance, garbage pickup, phones, insurance, business loans, vehicle loans, equipment loans, association dues, software, advertising, and so on.

2.) Variable Expenses

These are expenses that will change depending on the number of sales. When calculating gross profit, it only includes our variable costs. Some examples are cost of goods, commissions, packaging, shipping, and so on.

With simple math, we can understand that when we grow our sales, when our revenues go up, our variable expenses will go up. For me, it's easier to look at my gross profit margin. The gross profit margin is simply revenue minus variable expenses divided by revenue, times 100. For instance, if our revenue is $1,000,000 and our variable expenses are $700,000, that makes our gross profit $300,000. Then we divide that by our $1,000,000 in revenue and we get .30, then we times that by 100, which gives us a gross profit margin of 30 percent. Looking at the numbers from the expenses point of view, our variable costs are 70 percent.

For the P.R.O.S.P.E.R. Formula, we don't necessarily have to cut our variable expenses by 5 percent; that would be hard to do. We can, however, cut them by 2–3 percent fairly easily because of the economies of scale, which is a proportionate saving in costs gained by an increased level of production. For example, in most industries, we can increase sales by up to 10–15 percent and not have to hire another employee. We can also negotiate better pricing on the cost of goods with our vendors if we buy a larger volume.

Overall, we only need to decrease the total fixed and variable expenses by 5 percent NET.

IN THE TRENCHES
Five Ways to Decrease Expenses

1.) Billing Audit (Accounts Payable)

You must scrutinize your bank statement. Scrutinize means to examine or inspect closely and thoroughly. It's even more than a long, hard look. To scrutinize something, you must look at it really critically, investigate every minute detail. The verb for scrutinize is derived from the Latin word *scrutari*, which means "to search."

In business, we are to scrutinize things, not people. Every part of our monthly cashflow statement needs to be checked and questions asked. In my experience, there are always items that are "miscellaneous" and are too vague to decipher. The absolute best way to understand where your money is spent is to scrutinize every single transaction in your bank statement. The bank statement doesn't lie. In my agency, we have an accounts payable meeting once a quarter and going over every single transaction for the quarter.

At first it was a huge pain, because the name of the transaction did not match up to any vendor we recognized. Sometimes it would be the parent company name or a subsidiary. We would have to research it or call the company to figure out why we were giving them money. We now have a chart of who is who, so it's much easier. There have been more than a few times we could not figure out what the charge was for.

My business partner's philosophy is to cancel it and see what breaks or who squeals in 30 days. The funny thing is several times we have canceled things, and nothing happens; we just save money. Obviously the larger your company, the more transactions you will have, the more this will really help you cut expenses.

I promise if you truly scrutinize your bank statement, you will find several things you can cut immediately. It's amazing how many $47 a month things we can sign up for and then never use. These charges are not on our radar, because of how small the transaction is, but they add up to $564 a year.

Once you scrutinize your bank statement, what you will find are several things you are paying for that you probably don't want or need. For instance, during our audit, we sometimes find duplicates. These are things we are paying twice. It's easy to miss these because the bill is from an approved vendor and for the correct amount. If you sort by vendor and look at the past year, the discrepancies will pop out like a neon sign.

Second, you need to look to see if two different vendors do the same thing and whether you can cancel one of them. When we take on a new client, we make them give us a list of all the software they are buying. We always find things that they will no longer need because we are taking over that part of their marketing.

Last, vendors are far from perfect, and you would be amazed at how many times they make a billing mistake and charge more or less than they should. We have caught dozens of mistakes that we would have never found if we didn't scrutinize the bill for each vendor.

2.) Vendor Audit

Now that you have a detailed report of who you pay each month, it is time to negotiate. Thankfully, we always have options for most of our vendors. I am sure you learned just like I did, if you ever tried to cancel your cable bill, they amazingly have a new offer that is much cheaper if you stay. Well, you can negotiate dozens of things you spend money on each month. Here's is a partial list of some of the monthly expenditures that my business partner or I have negotiated or switched to a cheaper vendor and saved money.

- Phone bill
- Garbage bill
- Professional employer organization (PEO)
- Insurance
- Office supplies

- Shipping
- Repairs/maintenance
- Travel
- Tax preparation
- Website hosting
- Security monitoring
- Ink
- Call tracking
- Professional services
- Rent/mortgage rate
- Bad debts
- Credit card processing
- Marketing
- Booth space
- Promotional products

3.) Accounts Receivable

I put this under expenses because unless you only have a few customers, there is an exceedingly high probability you are not billing all your customers correctly. In my agency, we have a billing meeting once a quarter to go over each account and make sure we are billing them according to their contractual agreement.

It's startling how many times we sell a certain package to a client to charge them way less than what was agreed upon. There have also been a few times we charged them way too much. This can go on for months or years. It's likely your customer is not going to say anything because they do not do vendor audits. I'm embarrassed to say that we had a few clients that we did several months of work, and that we never charged them a penny. It's more common than you realize, and again, the larger the company, the higher the probability that mistakes are happening.

4.) Payroll

Except for maybe the cost of goods, your payroll is by far your biggest expense. I learned a long time ago that your business can only be as successful as your employees. I am certainly not recommending you cut anyone's pay or their benefits. However, it's extremely easy to tighten up your payroll by trimming the edges. Here are a few simple things you can implement that will save you money immediately.

No Unapproved Overtime

Overtime drastically increases your average payroll hour. For a simplistic example, if you have ten employees making $15 an hour, your payroll hour is $150. For a forty-hour work week, you pay $6,000, not including tax, worker's comp, unemployment, and so on. If you allow just an hour of overtime per employee, your weekly pay goes up $75 a week. If you allow that all year, that's an unnecessary extra $3900.

I get a lot of pushback when I tell the business owners to stop the overtime. They say, "They can't get it all done in 40 hours." My answer is then you need to hire another employee at $15 an hour. It's much cheaper than time and a half at $22.50 an hour. However, I'm willing to wager that 98 percent of the time, they can still get everything done in 40 hours. You will be amazed that things just get done quicker, which leads me to the next way to cut expenses.

Milking the Clock

In 1955, British naval historian and author Cyril Northcote Parkinson wrote an essay for *The Economist* in which the opening line read, "It is a commonplace observation that work expands so as to fill the time available for its completion." This later became known as Parkinson's Law. Parkinson is absolutely correct. If you pay your employees hourly, they will fill the time allotted. My award shop is extremely seasonal, and a few times a year our number of orders triple.

When we first bought the shop, we inherited a longtime employee who did the rotary engraving. During the busy season, he would get all the orders done and clock in right around 40 hours a week. What was odd was that in the summer when we had one-third the orders, he would clock in right around 40 hours a week. How could that be? I never once saw him screwing around or not working.

So, I started watching closer. Unfortunately, he didn't use the extra time to clean or do maintenance on the machines or any other proactive work. He simply did each order as usual, only slower. It's our job as managers to make sure there is enough work for the allotted hours, or we need to send workers home early. We cannot rely on our employees to "find something productive to do."

Another clock milking issue is bathroom breaks. Unfortunately, according to OSHA sanitation standards, you cannot tell an employee how long they can be in the bathroom or how many times a day they can go. There is not a federal standard for the number of restroom breaks allowed or length of time. There is no law against an employer denying restroom breaks. However, if they do, it could lead to lawsuits, and it's not worth that. We all know that 20- to 30-minute bathroom breaks are way too long and there is probably a phone involved. I have no fix for this. If you do, let me know. We can, however, scrutinize all other times of idleness.

About ten years ago, I installed a security system with cameras and access control. The back door would beep when someone went out the door and came back in. I had two employees who worked in production who took "random" smoke breaks throughout the day. The door beeps allowed me to track it.

For years, I never said anything because I thought it was only a couple times a day. Come to find out, they were out smoking 12–15 times a day. It was never exceedingly long, five to seven minutes, but that adds up to over an hour a day each, that I was paying for them to shorten their lives. I did not want to be an ogre, but I certainly was not going to pay for their smoke breaks anymore, so we made a new policy.

I said, if your work is caught up, you can take as many smoke breaks as you need; however, you must clock out. Amazingly, the smoke breaks were cut down by two-thirds per day, and they were not on my dime.

5.) Other Ways to Save Money

- Minimize software licenses to only what you need
- New, more efficient equipment (printers, AC, lights, etc.)
- Buyers group: buy larger volume as a group and save
- Rewards credit cards
- Senior/military/chamber discounts
- Anything charging interest should go away as soon as possible
- Annual pay versus monthly—often, if you pay the entire year in advance, you can save up to two months
- Save on electricity
  - o Programmable thermostat
  - o New LED lighting inside and outside our building—the savings made will usually pay for the costs of installation in less than six months
- Barter

You can barter just about anything. You can either trade straight across or join a barter network like ITEX, IMS Barter, or Barterco. The networks charge a transaction fee, usually around 12 percent, so it is imperative that you do the math. For us, our labor is 25 percent of our gross revenue. We don't barter Google or Facebook Ads spend, only our management fees. So, if we trade $1,000, our true hard cost is somewhere around $370, which is our labor costs plus the barter fees. The way I see it is I'm buying these things 37 cents on the dollar. Yes, you still must pay your taxes on the trade sales.

Here are a few things we buy on trade:

- Water cooler
- Weekly pizza for the staff
- Full catered meal for all staff meetings once a month
- Various restaurants
- Coffee shops
- Wine
- Christmas party
- Plants and moss walls throughout our office
- Flowers for special occasions
- Ink and toner
- Maid services
- Lawn maintenance
- Exterminator
- Tree service
- Pressure washing
- Clinic for tests (COVID, drug, etc.), bloodwork, flu shots, vitamin B-12 shots, etc.
- Dentists
- Eye doctor and glasses
- Advertising, radio, TV, cable, direct mail, magazines, billboards
- Printing
- Signs
- Photography
- Bookkeeping services
- VOIP phones
- Security alarm system and monitoring
- Condominiums stays
- Vacation trips
- Electricians
- Plumbers
- Auto repair (labor only)
- T-shirts with our logo

My experience in working with entrepreneurs is that most of them would rather lick the underbelly of a gecko than actually scrutinize their expenses. Before COVID, I had dozens of business owners tell me they were running lean and could not cut any more. Once COVID hit, they miraculously cut even more; we all did. What if we actually saved money on expenses without there being a global pandemic?

Fortunately, in the P.R.O.S.P.E.R. Formula, we only need to cut expenses by 5 percent. This is a critical step in the formula because it goes directly to your bottom line.

CHAPTER 20

(R) RETENTION
(Increase Your Retention by 5 Percent)

Retention is the new acquisition.
—Eddy Hill

30K FOOT VIEW

After we work so hard to get a customer, so few SMBs (small and medium-sized businesses) actually spend any time trying to keep those customers. Your customers have more choices than ever. Why should they continue to do business with you versus a local or online competitor, or anything at all?

Depending on what industry you are in, and which study you believe, acquiring a new customer is anywhere from 5 to 25 times more expensive than retaining an existing one. That's an astonishing stat. The same studies show that a mere 5 percent increase in customer retention can boost your bottom line by 25 to 95 percent.

A study by 1st Financial Training Services found that 96 percent of unhappy customers don't complain; however, 91 percent of those will simply leave and never come back.

One of the most powerful key performance indicators (KPIs) that a small business must keep track of is the retention rate. The retention rate is the percentage of customers who stayed with your company for a particular period of time. The other way you can calculate the KPI is the customer churn rate. This is a metric that measures the percentage of customers who end their relationship with your company in a particular period. Unfortunately, both of these metrics are lagging indicators, meaning you can only look at what has happened.

To increase our retention, we must understand the reasons customers leave. According to the book *Lessons from the Field* by Howard Feiertag and John Hogan, there are six basic reasons customers leave and never come back. They are referencing the hospitality industry, but I think this is absolutely relevant to all industries.

Why Do We Lose Customers?

- One percent die.

    There is nothing we can do about that.
- Three percent move away.

    For local service businesses, there is nothing you can do about this either.
- Five percent get referred somewhere else by a friend or relative.

    It is almost impossible to compete with a close friend or relative. At least until that customer finds out your competitor is incompetent.
- Nine percent switch because of a better price or product.

    Interesting. Most business owners would argue that a higher percentage of people will leave you because of price. This is not a segment of customers we want to go after. If they buy from you because of price, they will leave you because of price.
- Fourteen percent switch because of product or service dissatisfaction.

Now this is a segment of customers we can do something about. According to a survey done by Emplifi, a leading customer experience platform, 15 percent of dissatisfied customers will switch companies from only one terrible experience. Another 68 percent will leave after two bad experiences. We can do our best to make sure they are satisfied with the product or service the first time, and we can certainly make sure they don't have a bad experience twice.

According to a survey from the White House Office of Consumer Affairs, a dissatisfied customer will tell between 9 and 15 people about their experience. Around 13 percent of dissatisfied customers tell more than 20 people.

- Sixty-eight percent leave because they felt unappreciated, unimportant, and taken for granted!

Look at that stat again. This is completely mind boggling to me. Over two-thirds of our customers leave us and never come back because they felt unimportant, unappreciated, and taken for granted. This stat completely solidifies the fact that people undoubtably do business with people they know, like, and trust. Everything we have been discussing in this book is about ways to get more people to know you and your business, and how to get them to like and trust you.

If you are interested in keeping customers, you must be interested in understanding how many customers leave and the underlying reasons that they are ending their relationship with you.

The first step to increasing your customer retention is calculating your retention rate. The other way you can do it is calculating your attrition rate, sometimes called your churn rate, which is how many customers leave you over a period of time.

The average attrition or churn rate for all industries is 16–37 percent. Retention rate by industry:

- Retail: 63%
- Banking: 75%
- Telecom: 78%
- IT: 81%
- Insurance: 83%
- Professional services: 84%
- Media: 84%

How to Calculate Retention

I realize that some of you business owners would rather light your nose hair on fire and crunch on a cockroach than do math every single month. But I strongly exhort you to make a habit of calculating your retention every single month. Remember, retention is the new acquisition. Here's the formula.

[(# Customers at end of period – # customers acquired during period) ÷ # customers at start of period] × 100

For example: Imagine you start the year with 20 customers, gain 5 new customers in the first quarter, and have 1 customer churn:
[(24 – 5) / 20)] × 100 = 95% retention.

Here's another example: You have 44 customers, you gain 12 new customers, and 13 customers churn:
[(43 – 12) / 44)] × 100 = 70% retention.

IN THE TRENCHES
Six Ways to Increase Customer Retention

We have gone into great detail in other areas of the book about how to get your prospects to know, like, and trust you, and eventually they will try your business. These same tactics directly apply to your current customers as well. You must continue to build and deepen your relationship with each customer. As we see in the study from the beginning of this chapter, most of the customers we lose are those who felt unimportant, unappreciated, and taken for granted. Specifically, here are a few things you should purposefully do to increase your retention.

1.) Customer Segmentation

Facebook is rumored to track and collect over 52,000 data points on every user. You probably don't need that many data points, but you absolutely should be segmenting your customers. If you have high ticket customers but a lower quantity, like in my agency, you should collect as much info as possible. We use a CRM (customer relationship management) software that allows us to keep track of all their information, and we can bring it up before we have a meeting with them, to remind us of all the details. We collect information on things like their birthday, spouse, kids, alma mater, favorite sports teams, year their business opened, notes from all our past meetings, and so on. This information is super handy to have and makes a huge impression when we can talk intelligently about them. You can also segment your customers into groups so you can send specific messages that talk directly to them. In my awards business, we are higher volume, so it's hard to get a bunch of detail from each customer; however, we can still easily segment them to basic groups. When my sales staff takes an order, it forces them to pick one of these categories.

- Corporate
- Schools (Pre, Elementary, Middle, High, Junior College, University, Trade)
- Government
- Military
- Religious (Churches, Temples)
- Nonprofit
- Sports

This allows me to send personalized targeted emails and direct mail that is specifically catered to them. One-size-fits-all style correspondence is not personal enough to help with customer retention. To increase retention and build a loyal customer base, you need to invoke those fuzzy, warm feelings that create connections.

According to a study done by Infosys, 74 percent of consumers get frustrated by content that is not relevant to their lives.[5] Your online conversion rate can improve by about 8 percent with personalized online consumer experiences.

2.) Newsletters

As I mention in Chapter 8, newsletters are a great way to get prospects to like you, as well as an excellent way to retain customers. They allow you to stay in front of them and remind them of all the great value your business brings. Plus, you can have a call to action to reengage them. (By the way, you should sign up for my newsletter at https://prosperousim.com/prosperouspartner.)

I have seen excellent newsletters from virtually all local business niches. There is probably a "done for you" service that you can subscribe to that will write an excellent newsletter for you. The key to newsletters is consistency.

---

[5] https://www.infosys.com/newsroom/press-releases/Documents/genome-research-report.pdf

Send out a quality newsletter at least once a month for a year, and I guarantee your retention will grow.

3.) Lagniappe

I learned about the Louisiana French tradition of lagniappe when I first moved to the south. The term lagniappe has been traced back to the Quechua word *yapay*. Loosely translated, it means a little something extra, something that was not expected. The key to its effectiveness is the "unexpected," and it is an excellent way to build goodwill and get your clients to stay with you longer. This is something you could easily do and immediately implement in your business.

Giving your current customers unexpected gifts is a fantastic way to increase retention. In the first tactic, we segmented our customers and learned a little about them. Now we can send an unexpected gift that means something specific to them. Powerful bonding happens when you send a gift that says "Roll Tide" or something about their favorite sports team. A friend of mine had tennis balls made with his customer's logo on them. This was much more than just a gift; it was specifically personalized to his customer, who is a huge tennis player.

In my award shop, we like to surprise our customers with an extra personalized gift. It could be a stainless steel travel mug or maybe a leatherette notebook with their name and logo on it. It's easy for us to throw it in because we already have their logo from their awards. This is a powerful deposit in the emotional bank account.

I love to brainstorm different lagniappe gifts that my marketing clients should give out. I have a plumber who gives their customers those Plink fizzy drain freshener balls that clean and deodorize the garbage disposal and freshens the entire room with a pleasant lemon scent.

I have a mortgage broker who gives a monogrammed cutting board to everyone who gets a mortgage. I have an accountant who gives out calculators with his logo on them.

There are several Realtors who give a photo frame with a photo of their clients in front of their new home. The frame is personalized with their name, the date they bought it, and the inscription, "Our New Home!"

I have a law firm client who holds a free lunch-and-learn workshop for dozens of people each year to talk about insurance premiums from the legal point of view and not the insurance company's point of view. Financial advisors have been buying steak dinners for decades because it works to get new clients.

A friend of mine owns an extraordinarily successful auto glass company. Unfortunately, that industry has been extremely commoditized since insurance pays for most or all the windshields, so out-of-pocket costs are zero. What could be better than free? Well, he gives them a box of what he says are "really good steaks" with every window replacement just to say thanks for doing business with them. Brilliant! His mascot is a cow, and you will see him (the cow, not usually the owner) dancing around at the local baseball and hockey games. To propagate even more word of mouth, they have a "refer a friend" program where he gives a box of steaks for every referral that gets a new windshield. His word of mouth and referrals are through the roof, and it's impossible not to like him better than all the other glass companies in town. Their customer service is excellent, and they do splendid work. The likelihood of repeat business is almost 100 percent.

In my marketing agency, for every new client we sign up, we send out a huge, full, colored box that has our logos all over and "WELCOME" on the sides. When they open it, the gifts are beautifully presented with tissue paper and a heartfelt letter from me, welcoming them. All the gifts are personalized with their logo and some of them have "Courtesy of Prosperous Internet Marketing, Inc." We send them stainless steel travel mugs, premium leatherette pad folders, two high-end pens, a business card holder, a flashlight, and other trinkets. For our home services and shipping clients, we give them a tape measure with their logo on it, which is always a hit.

The gift we get the most feedback about is a 4" × 4" leatherette box that has their logo on top. When they open it, there is a 3-inch round button that says "Turn over to see an awesome lawyer" (or accountant or chiropractor, plumber or whatever their niche). On the other side is a mirror. Yes, I am well aware of how cheesy this is, in fact it's like Velveeta cheese—it's not even real cheese. However, this cheesy box usually stays on their desk for all to see and they are reminded of my company. Our customer retention rate is 15–20 percent higher than the industry standard, partly because of these gifts.

What is a little something extra that you can give your customer that is not expected?

4.) Ask for Feedback

This tactic is easy to do, but less than 5 percent of all businesses actually do it. No matter what the success of your business, there's always room for improvement. Some of the best ideas for making your products, processes, and customer service better will come from your customers. It's hard to read the label from the inside of the bottle. Some of your flaws can only be seen from the outside.

Customers stop doing business with you for a reason. Your job is to figure out why. Customer surveys can help. Providing customers with an opportunity to give feedback through surveys brings your business more insight into its operations. When you find a problem that happens over and over, fix it! When customers see the business taking their suggestions into account, and doing something about it, they have a feeling of ownership. This can create loyal customers who return again and again.

5.) Reengage with Inactive Customers

If you have been in business for a while, you probably have a huge database of customers who have bought from you in the past. Depending on how often your customers buy from you, a lot of these customers may be inactive, and you don't even know it. You can set up a reactivation campaign to remind them of your business. All they may need is a slight push from your side to make a repeat purchase. You can do this by offering them a discount, gift with purchase, or just something for free. We have an oil change client who pulls a report with every customer who hasn't purchased from them in the past 13 months. They send a cute postcard that says "Miss you! We have not seen you in a while! Was it something we said or did?" On the other side it has a large discount offer. They then follow up with an email and phone call. You could easily do the same with your customers that have been AWOL. Once you get a hold of them, it is important for you to improve your relationships with them and then find out why they left.

6.) Pain of Disconnect

This tactic may seem a bit nefarious; however, most of the time it's not even consciously done on purpose. As we well know, most people will take the path of least resistance. Some things are just a huge pain to cancel and change over to a new vendor, so we don't. Remember what Dr. John Townsend said: "Until the pain of staying the same is worse than the pain of change, people won't change."

A friend of mine absolutely hates his bank, but he won't switch because he doesn't want to go through the pain of getting new credit cards, new checks, and so on, so he stays.

I have a love/hate relationship with my order management software in my award shop. I thought of jumping ship dozens of times over the past ten years, but I cannot bring myself to leave because I have ten years of customer history, and the time for my entire staff to learn a new system would be a huge pain to move and not worth it.

In my agency, all the leads that we generate from the marketing we do for our clients go through tracking phone numbers. Our tracking numbers have what is called a "whisper." When our client answers the phone, they hear "Lead from Prosperous IM." Some of our clients hear it dozens of times per day. They know if they cancel, all those phone calls go away when we stop marketing.

Steve Jobs is the godfather of establishing the pain of disconnect. Apple products are purposefully not compatible with anything else. Once you start using Apple, there is no turning back without major pain. If you move over to an Android phone, you will lose all your apps, music, and even your chargers and earbuds won't work. Apple loves to brag about their retention rate, but I think it is because their customers are held hostage.

This is the last ingredient in the P.R.O.S.P.E.R. Formula. Retention has a profound effect on your profit. Remember, in today's economy, retention is the new acquisition.

The power of the formula lies not in one single ingredient. The power comes from compounding, from the exponential little bits. If you do any four of the seven ingredients in the P.R.O.S.P.E.R. Formula and increase them by a minimum of 5 percent (or decrease in the case of expenses), it will double your profit.

In the appendix, I give you sample businesses that implemented the P.R.O.S.P.E.R. Formula and the result. You can see the math and how the formula works.

If you want to plug in your own numbers, go to http://prosperformula. com/resources and download the cashflow spreadsheet.

CHAPTER 21

CONCLUSION

I started this book with the four circles of success, Mindset, Skill Set, Toolset, and Get Off Your Asset.

In every chapter in this book, we covered the 30,000-foot, high-level, overview, which hopefully got you in the right mindset of why you need to do it, then I went deep in the trenches on the skills, the specific tactical steps you need to implement in your business, and I referenced dozens of specific tools you can use to shortcut your success.

In the second section of this book, I thoroughly went through the customer journey of Know, Like, Trust, Try, Buy, and Evangelize, and exactly how to purposefully move people along that journey.

I concluded this book with the third section, the P.R.O.S.P.E.R. Formula, covering the exact steps on how to double your profit and significantly grow your business.

The only thing I didn't do for you in this book is implement. It's time for you to Get Off Your Asset and take some massive action. Remember, an object in motion tends to stay in motion. The absolute best time to take action is the day after yesterday, and the second best is the day before tomorrow.

Start with a quick win, go after the low hanging fruit, and get in motion. You will start seeing results, then the upward spiral will kick in and motivate you to keep taking action. Keep moving forward, "That's how winning is done!"

If you need directions on what to do first, take my free business assessment survey https://prosperformula.com/assessment. This will blatantly point out your weaknesses and show you which area will have the biggest impact on your business. If you hit a wall, and just cannot seem to make the improvement you want, schedule a strategy session with one of our elite P.R.O.S.P.E.R. coaches, and we will be glad to give you a proposal for us to implement all these tactics for you. Https://prosperformula.com/strategy.

Go forth and prosper ... oh, and live long too!

> *Beloved, I wish above all things that thou mayest pros-*
> *per and be in health, even as thy soul prospereth.*
> *—III John 1:2*

APPENDIX

The appendix is to help you to see math and the power of the exponential little bits (ELBs), the power of each ingredient compounding in the P.R.O.S.P.E.R. Formula. Go ahead and check the math, but make sure you do it in order: start with the prospects, then ratio of closed sales, then order average, then sales frequency, then retention if applicable. I did not add anything for productivity in these examples because it's hard to quantify. But make no mistake, increased productivity will absolutely show up in your profit.

Calculator Emoji Accounting Firm

Income Statement

Address: 123 Street Avenue, Cityville, State, 12333

Income Statement

Revenue	Year 1	Year 2	
Sales	$1,000,000.00	$1,158,150.00	
Net Sales	$1,000,000.00	$1,158,150.00	
(Variable Costs)	20%	20%	
CPA Distributions, Override, Bonus, Profit Share	$200,000.00	$231,630.00	
Total Variable Costs	$200,000.00	$231,630.00	
Gross Profit	$800,000.00	$926,520.00	
Operating Expenses (Fixed Costs)			
CPA Salaries/Wages	$370,000.00	$370,000.00	
Other Salaries/Wages	$200,000.00	$197,000.00	
Advertising	$48,000.00	$48,000.00	
Repairs & Maintenance	$7,500.00	$6,000.00	
Travel	$7,500.00	$6,500.00	
Rent/Mortgage	$48,000.00	$48,000.00	
Delivery/Freight Expenses	$2,000.00	$1,800.00	
Utilities/Telephone Expenses	$8,500.00	$8,300.00	
Insurance	$3,500.00	$3,200.00	
Mileage	$1,500.00	$1,400.00	
Office Supplies	$2,500.00	$2,100.00	
Other Expenses	$1,000.00	$700.00	
Total Operating Expenses	$700,000.00	$693,000.00	
Operating Profit (Loss)	$100,000.00	$233,520.00	
Add: Other Income			
Interest Income	$0.00	$0.00	
Other Income	$0.00	$0.00	
Profit (Loss) Before Taxes	$100,000.00	$233,520.00	5% Tax Savings
Less: Income Tax Expense	$25,000.00	$55,461.00	(25%* .95=23.75%)
Net Profit (Loss)	$75,000.00	$178,059.00	
	Net Profit Increase	$103,059.00	

Calculator Emoji CPA

Gross Sales	$1,000,000.00		$1,158,150.00	
Customers Closed	1000		1103	50% Close Ratio to 52.50% Close Ratio
Total Prospects	2000		2100	5% Increase
Retention	75%		78.75%	
Average Order	$1,000.00		$1,050.00	5% Increase
Variable Expenses	$200,000.00	20% of Gross Sales	$231,630.00	20% of Gross Sales
GROSS PROFIT	$800,000.00		$926,520.00	
Fixed Expenses	$700,000.00		$693,000.00	1% Decrease
Net Profit	$100,000.00		$233,520.00	Net Increase $133,520.00

Assumptions

4 - Partners
2 - Entry-Level CPAs
5 - Support Staff

PROSPER FORMULA INGREDIENTS USED

Prospects	5% Increase
Ratio of Closed Sales	5% Increase
Order Average	5% Increase
Sales Frequency	=
Productivity	>
Variable Expenses	=
Fixed Expenses	1% Decrease
Retention	>

Dog Emoji Veterinarian — Income Statement

Address: 123 Street Avenue, Cityville, State, 12333

Income Statement

Revenue	Year 1	Year 2
Sales	$1,000,000.00	$1,212,915.90
Net Sales	$1,000,000.00	$1,212,915.90
(Variable Costs)	25%	23.75%
Materials/Supplies	$250,000.00	$288,067.53
Total Variable Costs	$250,000.00	$288,067.53
Gross Profit	$750,000.00	$924,848.37
Operating Expenses (Fixed Costs)		
Veterinarian Salaries/ Wages	$350,000.00	$350,000.00
Veterinarian Technician Saleries/ Wages	$125,000.00	$125,000.00
Other Salaries/ Wages	$35,000.00	$35,000.00
Advertising	$36,000.00	$36,000.00
Repairs & Maintenance	$12,000.00	$10,000.00
Travel	$5,000.00	$4,250.00
Rent/Mortgage	$60,000.00	$60,000.00
Delivery/Freight Expenses	$2,000.00	$1,750.00
Utilities/Telephone Expenses	$7,500.00	$7,000.00
Insurance	$7,500.00	$7,000.00
Mileage	$2,500.00	$2,000.00
Office Supplies	$6,500.00	$5,000.00
Other Expenses	$1,000.00	$500.00
Total Operating Expenses	$650,000.00	$643,500.00
Operating Profit (Loss)	$100,000.00	$281,348.37
	Net Increase	$181,348.37

Dog Emoji Veterinarian

Gross Sales	$1,000,000.00		$1,212,915.90	
Customers Closed	4000		4409	90% Close Ratio to 94.5% Close Ratio
Total Prospects	4444		4666	5% Increase
Average Sales Frequency	1.25		1.31	5% Increase
Average Spend per Year	$240		$275.10	Average Order × Average Freq
Retention	75%		79%	
Average Order	$200.00		$210.00	5% Increase
Variable Expenses	$250,000.00	25%	$288,067.53	23.75% of Gross Sales - 5%
GROSS PROFIT	$750,000.00		$924,848.37	Gross Profit Margin (76.25%)
Fixed Expenses	$650,000.00		$643,500.00	1% Decrease
Net Profit	$100,000.00		$281,348.37	**Net Increase** **$181,348.37**

Assumptions

Open 6 Days a Week (Mon–Sat)

6 Holidays a Year

2 Full-Time Veterinarians

2 Full-Time Vet Techs

2 Part-Time Vet Techs

1 Full-Time Receptionist

PROSPER FORMULA INGREDIENTS USED

Prospects	5% Increase
Ratio of Closed Sales	5% Increase
Order Average	5% Increase
Sales Frequency	5% Increase
Productivity	>
Expenses Variable	5% Decrease
Expenses Fixed	1% Decrease
Retention	>

Poop Emoji Plumbing

Income Statement

Address: 123 Street Avenue, Sewerville, State, 12333

Income Statement

Revenue	Year 1	Year 2
Sales	$1,000,000.00	$1,157,625.00
Net Sales	**$1,000,000.00**	**$1,157,625.00**
Cost of Goods Sold (Variable Costs)	55%	52.25%
Materials/Supplies	$240,000.00	$264,000.00
Tech Wages/ Commissions	$310,000.00	$340,859.06
Total Cost of Goods Sold	**$550,000.00**	**$604,859.06**
Gross Profit	**$450,000.00**	**$552,765.94**
Operating Expenses (Fixed Costs)		
Other Salaries/ Wages	$247,000.00	$235,000.00
Advertising	$60,000.00	$59,000.00
Repairs & Maintenance, Equipment	$9,500.00	$8,300.00
Travel	$5,000.00	$4,500.00
Rent/Mortgage	$24,000.00	$22,500.00
Delivery/Freight Expenses	$1,000.00	$950.00
Utilities/Telephone Expenses	$4,600.00	$3,500.00
Insurance	$3,500.00	$3,200.00
Mileage/Gas	$6,500.00	$6,200.00
Office Supplies	$1,000.00	$800.00
Other Expenses	$900.00	$900.00
Total Operating Expenses	**$363,000.00**	**$344,850.00**
Operating Profit (Loss)	**$87,000.00**	**$207,915.94**
	Net Increase	**$120,915.94**

Poop Emoji Plumber

Gross Sales	$1,000,000.00	$1,157,625.00	
Customers Closed	2000	2205	80% Closing Ratio to 84%
Total Prospects	2500	2625	5% Increase
Average Order	$500.00	$525.00	5% Increase
Variable Expenses	$550,000.00 55% of Gross Sales	$604,859.06	52.25% of Gross Sales (-5%)
GROSS PROFIT	$450,000.00	$552,765.94	
Fixed Expenses	$363,000.00	$344,850.00	5% Decrease
Net Profit	$87,000.00	$207,915.94	Net Increase $120,915.94

PROSPER FORMULA INGREDIENTS USED

Prospects	5% Increase
Ratio of Closed Sales	5% Increase
Order Average	5% Increase
Sales Frequency	=
Productivity	>
Expenses	5% Decrease
Retention	>

Assumptions

Owner Works in the Business
2 - Full-Time Technicians   2 Trucks
1 - Technician in Training
1 - Customer Service Rep

Restaurant Emoji Italian

Address: 123 Street Avenue, Cityville, State, 12333

Income Statement

Income Statement

Revenue	Year 1	Year 2
Sales	$1,200,000.00	$1,411,200.00
Net Sales	**$1,200,000.00**	**$1,411,200.00**
Cost of Goods Sold (Variable Costs)	**40%**	**40%**
Food/Materials/Supplies	$480,000.00	$564,480.00
Total Cost of Goods Sold	**$480,000.00**	**$564,480.00**
Gross Profit	**$720,000.00**	**$846,720.00**
Operating Expenses (Fixed Costs)		
Owner Salaries/Wages	$100,000.00	$100,000.00
Other Salaries/Wages	$350,000.00	$346,000.00
Advertising	$50,000.00	$50,000.00
Repairs, Maintenance, Equipment	$33,000.00	$30,000.00
Travel	$7,500.00	$5,250.00
Rent/Mortgage	$96,000.00	$96,000.00
Delivery/Freight Expenses	$8,000.00	$7,000.00
Utilities/Telephone Expenses	$15,000.00	$14,000.00
Insurance	$7,500.00	$7,000.00
Mileage	$1,000.00	$560.00
Office Supplies	$2,500.00	$2,000.00
Other Expenses	$1,500.00	$750.00
Total Operating Expenses	**$672,000.00**	**$658,560.00**
Operating Profit (Loss)	**$48,000.00**	**$188,160.00**
	Net Increase	**$140,160.00**

Restaurant Emoji Italian Restaurant

Gross Sales	$1,200,000.00	$1,411,200.00	
Unique Customers per Year	2000	2100	5% Increase
Average Sales Frequency	15	16	5% Increase
Average Visit Costs	$40	$42	5% Increase
Average Spend per Year	$600	$672.00	
Retention	80%	84%	
Average Order	$40.00	$42.00	5% Increase
Variable Expenses	$480,000.00	40% of Gross Sales	$564,480.00	40% of Gross Sales
GROSS PROFIT	$720,000.00	$846,720.00	
Fixed Expenses	$672,000.00	$658,560.00	2% Decrease
Net Profit	**$48,000.00**	**$188,160.00**	**Net Increase**	**$140,160.00**

Italian Restaurant

		PROSPER FORMULA INGREDIENTS USED	
20 Booths That Seat 4		Prospects	5% Increase
5 Tables That Seat 6		Ratio of Closed Sales	5% Increase
Full Bar		Order Average	5% Increase
Open 360 Days a Year	11a-10p	Sales Frequency	5% Increase
		Productivity	>
		Variable Expenses	=
		Fixed Expenses	2% Decrease
		Retention	>

Scale Emoji Law Firm
Address: 123 Street Avenue, Lawville, State, 12333

Income Statement

Income Statement

Revenue	Year 1	Year 2
Retainers	$240,000.00	$327,600.00
Billable Hours	$400,000.00	$441,000.00
Other Income	$110,000.00	$115,500.00
Sales	**$750,000.00**	**$884,100.00**
(Variable Costs)	**25%**	**23.75%**
Attorney Distributions, Override, Bonus, Profit Share	$150,000.00	$167,979.00
Court Filing Fees, Witness Fees, Laboratory Fees, Deposition Fees	$37,500.00	$41,995.00
Total Variable Expenses	**$187,500.00**	**$209,974.00**
Gross Profit	**$562,500.00**	**$674,126.00**
Operating Expenses (Fixed Costs)		
Attorney Salaries/ Wages	$200,000.00	$200,000.00
Other Salaries/Wages	$160,000.00	$160,000.00
Advertising	$60,000.00	$60,000.00
Travel	$12,000.00	$10,500.00
Rent/Mortgage	$48,000.00	$48,000.00
Delivery/Freight Expenses	$5,000.00	$4,500.00
Utilities/Telephone Expenses	$12,500.00	$11,500.00
Insurance	$5,500.00	$4,500.00
Mileage	$3,000.00	$2,000.00
Office Supplies	$3,500.00	$2,800.00
Other Expenses	$2,000.00	$1,000.00
Total Operating Expenses	**$511,500.00**	**$504,800.00**
Operating Profit (Loss)	**$51,000.00**	**$169,326.00**
	Net Increase	**$118,326.00**

Scale Emoji Law Firm

	Last Year	This Year	
GROSS SALES	$750,000.00	$884,100.00	
Total Retainer Fees	$240,000.00	$327,600.00	
Clients on Retainer	20	18	89% Retention Rate
Average Retainer Fee per Year	$12,000.00	$12,600.00	5% Increase
Total Prospects for Retainer	14	15	5% Increase
Total New Clients on Retainers	7	8	50% Closing Ratio to 52.50% Closing Ratio
Billable Hours Total Fees	$400,000.00	$441,000.00	
Average Hourly Rate	$200	$210.00	Increase Hourly Rate 5%
Total Billable Hours	2000	2100	5% More Billable Hours
Other Income	$110,000.00	$115,500.00	5% Increase
Variable Expenses	$187,500.00	$209,974.00	23.75% of Gross Sales
GROSS PROFIT	$562,500.00	$674,126.00	
Fixed Expenses	$511,500.00	$504,800.00	2% Decrease
Net Profit	$51,000.00	$169,326.00	Net Increase $118,326.00

Note on Variable Expenses (Last Year): 25% of Gross Sales

Assumtions

2 - Partner Lawyers	
1 - Associate Lawyer	
2 - Paralegals	
1 - Receptionist	

PROSPER FORMULA INGREDIENTS USED

Prospects (MRR)	5% Increase
Ratio of Closed Sales	5% Increase
Order Average	5% Increase
Sales Frequency (Billable Hours)	5% Increase
Productivity	>
Variable Expenses	5% Decrease
Fixed Expenses	2% Decrease
Retention	89%

Smiley Emoji Photography

Address: 123 Street Avenue, Cityville, State, 12333

Income Statement

Income Statement

Revenue	Year 1	Year 2
Sales	$200,000.00	$232,050.00
Net Sales	$200,000.00	$232,050.00
Cost of Goods Sold (Variable Costs)	50%	47.50%
Materials/Supplies	$10,000.00	$10,223.75
Photographer	$90,000.00	$100,000.00
Total Cost of Goods Sold	$100,000.00	$110,223.75
Gross Profit	$100,000.00	$121,826.25
Operating Expenses (Fixed Costs)		
Other Salaries/Wages	$30,000.00	$28,500.00
Advertising	$12,000.00	$12,000.00
Repairs, Maintenance, Equipmnet	$10,000.00	$9,000.00
Travel	$8,000.00	$7,800.00
Memberships/Education	$500.00	$450.00
Printing	$5,000.00	$4,800.00
Delivery/Freight Expenses	$500.00	$450.00
Utilities/Telephone Expenses	$1,500.00	$1,400.00
Insurance	$2,750.00	$2,500.00
Mileage/Gas	$3,500.00	$3,400.00
Office Supplies	$250.00	$200.00
Other Expenses	$1,000.00	$750.00
Total Operating Expenses	$75,000.00	$71,250.00
Operating Profit (Loss)	$25,000.00	$50,576.25
	Net Increase	$25,576.25

Smiley Emoji Photographer

Gross Sales	$200,000.00	$232,050.00	
Customers Closed	200	221	80% Close Ratio to 84% Close Ratio
Total Prospects	250	263	5% Increase
Average Order	$1,000.00	$1,050.00	5% Increase
Variable Expenses	$100,000.00 50%	$110,223.75	47.5% Variable expenses
GROSS PROFIT	$100,000.00 50% Gross Profit	$121,826.25	Gross Profit Margin 52.5%
Fixed Expenses	$75,000.00	$71,250.00	5% Decrease
Net Profit	$25,000.00	$50,576.25	Net Increase $25,576.25

PROSPER FORMULA INGREDIENTS USED

Prospects	5% Increase
Ratio of Closed Sales	5% Increase
Order Average	5% Increase
Sales Frequency	=
Productivity	>
Expenses	5% Decrease
Retention	>

Assumptions
1 Full-Time Photographer
1 Part-Time Assistant

Trophy Cup Emoji Award
Address: 123 Street Avenue, Cityville, State, 12333

Income Statement

Income Statement

Revenue	Year 1	Year 2
Sales	$500,000.00	$606,457.95
Net Sales	$500,000.00	$606,457.95
Cost of Goods Sold (Variable Costs)	40%	38.80%
Materials/Supplies	$200,000.00	$235,305.68
Total Cost of Goods Sold	$200,000.00	$235,305.68
Gross Profit	$300,000.00	$371,152.27
Operating Expenses (Fixed Costs)		
Owner Salaries/Wages	$70,000.00	$70,000.00
Other Salaries/Wages	$66,000.00	$66,000.00
Advertising	$24,000.00	$24,000.00
Repairs, Maintenance, Equipment	$16,000.00	$13,650.00
Travel	$5,000.00	$4,000.00
Rent/Mortgage	$48,000.00	$48,000.00
Delivery/Freight Expenses	$12,000.00	$10,500.00
Utilities/Telephone Expenses	$16,000.00	$14,800.00
Insurance	$3,500.00	$3,000.00
Mileage	$1,500.00	$1,000.00
Office Supplies	$2,000.00	$1,500.00
Other Expenses	$1,000.00	$600.00
Total Operating Expenses	$265,000.00	$257,050.00
Operating Profit (Loss)	$35,000.00	$114,102.27
Net Increase		$79,102.27

Trophy Cup Emoji Award Shop

Gross Sales	$500,000.00	$606,457.95	
Customers Closed	4000	4409	90% Closing Ratio to 94.5% Closing Ratio
Total Prospects	4444	4666	5% Increase
Sales Frequency	1.25	1.31	5% Increase
Average Order	$100.00	$105.00	5% Increase
Variable Expenses	$200,000.00	40%	$235,305.69	38.8% Variable Expenses (40% .97)
GROSS PROFIT	$300,000.00		$371,152.26	
Fixed Expenses	$265,000.00		$257,050.00	3% Decrease
Net Profit	$35,000.00		$114,102.26	Net Increase $79,102.26

Assumptions

Open Monday–Friday

PROSPER FORMULA INGREDIENTS USED

Prospects	5% Increase
Ratio of Closed Sales	5% Increase
Order Average	5% Increase
Sales Frequency	5% Increase
Productivity	>
Variable Expenses	3% Decrease
Fixed Expenses	3% Decrease
Retention	>

Made in United States
Orlando, FL
27 April 2023

32538413R00111